"*The Bipolar Workbook for Teens* offers potent sup[illegible] disorder, empowering them with knowledge and practical tools for their journey towards self-acceptance and self-knowledge."

—Shirley Eyles, mental health nurse, certified Theraplay therapist in private practice, and coauthor of *Applications of Family and Group Theraplay*

"I highly recommend this excellent workbook, not only for teens diagnosed with bipolar disorder, but also for those experiencing troublesome mood swings. Readers will learn essential skills to manage symptoms. This workbook is user-friendly, well-organized, encouraging, and based in research."

—Francine Brill, MD, FRCP(C), child and adolescent psychiatrist at Southlake Regional Health Centre in Newmarket, ON, Canada

"The authors of this book speak directly to youth in a respectful and genuine manner. There is tremendous value in reading stories of other teens who have shared similar experiences. This book is truly a welcome addition to the educational resources available to adolescents who live with the complex difficulties of bipolar disorder."

—Janice Phillips, B.Ed., educator and mental health social worker

"This is an excellent, easy-to-read workbook for teens suffering from bipolar disorder. Teens will identify with the client scenarios shared in the book. It presents a straightforward approach to gaining knowledge about the illness, learning tools to help overcome symptoms, and practicing exercises to establish new thought patterns and behaviors. Used in conjunction with medication, the knowledge and exercises in this book will help teens prevent deterioration, take control of the symptoms of bipolar disorder, and optimize their quality of life."

—Linda Jeffery, RN, cognitive behavior therapist in private practice and manager of Crisis Services of the Canadian Mental Health Association, Simcoe County Branch

the bipolar workbook for teens

dbt skills to help you control **mood swings**

SHERI VAN DIJK, MSW
KARMA GUINDON, MSW

Instant Help Books
A Division of New Harbinger Publications, Inc.

Publisher's Note

This publication is designed to provide accurate and authoritative information in regard to the subject matter covered. It is sold with the understanding that the publisher is not engaged in rendering psychological, financial, legal, or other professional services. If expert assistance or counseling is needed, the services of a competent professional should be sought.

Distributed in Canada by Raincoast Books

Instant Help Books
A Division of New Harbinger Publications, Inc.
5674 Shattuck Avenue
Oakland, CA 94609
www.newharbinger.com

Cover design by Amy Shoup
Interior illustrations by Julie Olson

Printed in the United States of America

Library of Congress Cataloging-in-Publication Data

Van Dijk, Sheri.
The bipolar workbook for teens : DBT skills to help you control mood swings / Sheri Van Dijk, MSW and Karma Guindon.
p. cm.
ISBN-13: 978-1-57224-696-6 (pbk. : alk. paper)
ISBN-10: 1-57224-696-0 (pbk. : alk. paper)
ISBN-13: 978-1-57224-878-6 (pdf ebook)
ISBN-10: 1-57224-878-5 (pdf ebook)
1. Manic-depressive illness in adolescence--Popular works. 2. Dialectical behavior therapy--Popular works. I. Guindon, Karma. II. Title.
RJ506.D4V36 2010
616.89'500835--dc22

2009044373

12 11 10

10 9 8 7 6 5 4 3 2 1

First Printing

To all the young people diagnosed with bipolar disorder—be brave and have hope! Also, to my family and friends—thank you for your support, encouragement, and love.

—Sheri Van Dijk

To Bill, thank you for your love and support. To those of you who will use this workbook—bipolar disorder is not the whole story of you. There are many more.

—Karma Guindon

contents

✱ contents

introduction

Dear Reader,

If you bought or were given this book, you either have bipolar disorder or have been experiencing troublesome mood swings. Mood swings can have a severe impact on your life, preventing you from reaching long-term goals and having a negative effect on your relationships. There are skills you can learn to help you cope with your symptoms and have more control over your emotions. Working through this book can help you learn them.

The activities in this workbook are largely based on a treatment called dialectical behavior therapy (DBT), which was developed by Dr. Marsha Linehan, a psychologist and professor at the University of Washington, and is presented in her book *Cognitive-Behavioral Treatment of Borderline Personality Disorder* (New York: Guilford Press, 1993).

These activities will help you gain insight into your life and teach you skills that will help with your symptoms, but it's up to you to put those skills into practice. As you do each activity, give yourself time to really think about it and to learn each skill before moving on to the next.

This book is not meant to replace professional help. If your mood swings are quite troublesome and impact your ability to function—perhaps you stop going to school at times, or use substances or other less helpful coping skills to avoid your problems—you still need to seek help from a doctor and a psychotherapist. If you have bipolar disorder, you have likely been prescribed medications, and it's important that you remain on them and follow your doctor's instructions. If you have thoughts of suicide, please tell someone you trust immediately so that you can get the help you need.

Learning skills to help you manage your emotions and be more effective in your life is hard work. It means recognizing that some things you currently do aren't working very well, and looking at ways you can change those things. Some people have a tendency to be hard on themselves when they have trouble making changes or when they fall back on old patterns even after they've been learning and practicing new ones. But remember: change is always hard! So as you go through this workbook, make sure you regularly give yourself a pat on the back for the hard work you are doing, and congratulate yourself for taking the steps to live a healthier, happier life.

a look at your bipolar symptoms

1

for you to know

Bipolar disorder is a very unpredictable condition that makes your mood go up and down a lot. Sometimes you might feel really down or depressed, and at other times you might feel incredibly good about yourself, like you could do anything you set your mind to. At still other times, you might feel like you have a lot of energy but can't sit still and often feel angry or annoyed.

When he was thirteen, Jamie began to have periods of time when he felt so down that he withdrew from his family and friends. He would hide away in his bedroom whenever he could. Although he still went to school, getting up in the morning became really hard, and he had no energy at the end of the day to do homework or even to do fun things that he used to enjoy, like playing video games. Concentrating was also really hard, and before long, Jamie's grades were falling and his parents were getting phone calls from the school. When his parents tried to talk to him about it, Jamie would get so angry that he could barely think straight. He would end up yelling at them and sometimes even throwing things. Later, he would feel so guilty and ashamed of his behavior that he would have thoughts of killing himself. His emotional pain was so strong that he just didn't want to be there anymore. Jamie's story shows some of the effects of depression.

Lindsay had been feeling really good for a few weeks; her energy level was high, and she was needing much less sleep than usual, which meant she was able to get a lot more stuff done. At school one day, she began to think about how much smarter she was than her teachers—she already knew what they were teaching her and thought she could do a better job than they were. She told her math teacher that and ended up with a detention after school. When Lindsay got home late, her mother asked her why. She responded that she didn't think she had to go to school anymore; she wasn't getting anything out of it that she didn't already know and she thought she'd speak to her guidance counselor about graduating early. When her mother questioned this, Lindsay became really angry and left the house in a rage. Lindsay's story is an example of a manic episode.

Camille had stopped taking her medication because she hated the numb feeling and other side effects it gave her. After a few days, she noticed that she was sleeping a bit less than usual and snapping more easily at little things that usually wouldn't bother her. She felt jumpy and kind of agitated, like she just couldn't sit still. She had all of this pent-up energy and didn't know what to do with it. On top of that, she was starting to feel depressed and to have thoughts about hurting herself. These thoughts frightened Camille enough that she admitted to her mom that she had stopped taking her meds, and they were able to get her help. Camille was experiencing a mixed episode, or symptoms of depression and mania at the same time.

The stories of Jamie, Lindsay, and Camille are examples of how depression, mania, and mixed episodes can affect you. Some manic episodes are full-blown and some are mild; mild episodes are known as hypomania. Throughout this book, we will use "mania" to refer to both types of episodes.

The symptoms of bipolar disorder are different for different people, and your own symptoms will vary from episode to episode. It's very important for you to get to know the symptoms you can experience during a bipolar episode. By noticing these symptoms as they appear, you'll be able to tell when you might be entering one of these states.

for you to do

The first list includes symptoms that a lot of people have when they feel depressed, and the second includes common symptoms of mania. Some of these symptoms can occur whether you're feeling depressed or manic, and, if you have mixed episodes, you might have symptoms of depression and mania at the same time. Check off any of the symptoms that you've had and use the blank lines to write down any others not on the list.

Symptoms of Depression

____ feeling very sad

____ feeling like you don't matter

____ changes in your sleep

____ feeling "empty"

____ hiding away from people

____ difficulty remembering things

____ decrease in energy

____ feeling hopeless

____ feeling restless

____ difficulty making decisions

____ thoughts of hurting yourself

____ eating more or less than usual

____ feeling angry a lot

____ weight changes

____ snapping at people more often

____ problems concentrating

____ thoughts of suicide

____ lack of interest in doing things

____ feeling helpless

____ crying a lot

____ not liking yourself

____ feeling guilty

____ loss of enjoyment in activities you used to like

Other changes you notice about yourself when you're feeling depressed:

______________________________ ______________________________

______________________________ ______________________________

______________________________ ______________________________

Symptoms of Mania

____ rapid, unpredictable emotional changes

____ scattered, confusing thoughts

____ doing many more activities than usual

____ feeling really good about yourself

____ spending more money than usual

____ having a lot more sexual feelings than usual

____ talking very fast

____ ignoring responsibilities (e.g., work, school)

____ feeling paranoid

____ eating less

____ poor judgment

____ thinking you can do things better than others

____ less need for sleep

____ having a lot more energy

____ feeling really happy

____ feeling irritable

____ driving fast or dangerously

____ having a hard time relaxing

____ using drugs or alcohol

____ lack of control

____ shoplifting

____ agitation

____ feeling really anxious

____ having intense nightmares

Other symptoms of mania you've experienced:

________________________________ ________________________________

________________________________ ________________________________

________________________________ ________________________________

Are there any symptoms you checked off that you weren't aware of before reading these lists? Write them here:

____

____

____

____

Did you check off symptoms that you were aware of but didn't know were related to your bipolar disorder? If so, what were they?

____

____

____

____

Every day this week, pull out both lists and review them. Notice if you are currently experiencing any of the symptoms you checked and if you need to check off others.

… and more to do

Here are some feelings other people have had when they learned that the symptoms mentioned earlier could be related to their bipolar disorder. Circle any that apply to you:

angry	sad	hopeful
relieved	surprised	overwhelmed
confident	afraid	acceptable

List other words that might describe your feelings about these symptoms and the fact that they could be related to your bipolar disorder:

__________________ __________________ __________________

__________________ __________________ __________________

For each emotion you circled or listed, briefly explain why you think you feel that way.

____

____

____

____

____

____

bipolar disorder also affects your family

2

for you to know

The bipolar symptoms you experience also affect the people around you. It can be very helpful for you to talk to your family and close friends about these symptoms and to ask for their help in monitoring them.

Kelly was in the middle of finals in his junior year of high school. He was determined to keep his grades up, which meant staying up late at night studying. After three nearly sleepless nights in a row, he was feeling confident about how well he would do and told his parents he was going to a friend's house for a party.

Kelly's parents shared their concern about his lack of sleep. They also mentioned that they were worried because he hadn't been eating very much over the last few days and had been more irritable toward his family. He hadn't noticed these other changes in himself, and he agreed with his parents' suggestion that this could be the onset of a manic episode. He needed a break from his studying so he went to his friend's party but returned home early to get some sleep and take care of himself.

for you to do

Look at yourself through the eyes of someone else (like a family member or friend). What symptoms of depression and mania might they say you experience?

___

___

___

Next, ask your family members what symptoms they see in you when you are depressed or manic. Write those symptoms here:

___

___

___

... and more to do

Try to pay attention the next time you're feeling depressed or manic and see if you can notice the changes your family described. Write about what you notice and see if your observations match what your family described.

3 a look at who else you are

for you to know

A chronic condition like bipolar disorder can be so overwhelming that it seems like it defines who you are. But you are not bipolar disorder, and bipolar disorder isn't you! You're a lot more than just someone with bipolar disorder.

At times, your bipolar disorder may make it harder for you to function as well as you'd like in different areas of your life, but you need to keep pursuing your dreams. It's very important to remind yourself that you have many qualities and characteristics that have nothing to do with bipolar disorder. This will help you to live your life in a more positive, healthy way so that you can work toward your goals and have a high quality of life in spite of the additional challenges you face because of your condition.

for you to do

In addition to being a son or daughter, you might also be a committed friend, a good listener, a poet or artist, a nature lover, and someone who accepts differences. You can probably find lots of things that make up who you are, other than being someone with bipolar disorder. Take some time to think about the qualities and skills you have and list them here.

______________ ______________ ______________

______________ ______________ ______________

______________ ______________ ______________

______________ ______________ ______________

Was it difficult for you to think of who you are and of your different qualities and skills? Ask some people you trust who they see you as. Write down their ideas.

______________ ______________ ______________

______________ ______________ ______________

______________ ______________ ______________

______________ ______________ ______________

Next, think about who you *want* to be. What kinds of things do you want for yourself? Do you want to get higher grades in school? Is there a sport or hobby you would like to pursue, or perhaps a personal quality or skill? Write any ideas you have here.

______________ ______________ ______________

______________ ______________ ______________

______________ ______________ ______________

______________ ______________ ______________

... and more to do

Over the next week, continue to think about the questions of who you are and who you would like to be. If you come up with other answers to this question, add them to your lists.

how your family and friends can help

4

for you to know

You're probably still getting used to what bipolar disorder means for your life, what it looks like, and what it can do. You're not alone in trying to figure these things out. You probably have family, friends, counselors, and health care professionals who care about you and want to help you. This is a great time for you to ask these people for help.

What you tell people in your life about your condition is going to vary. You may have some friends who will never know you have bipolar disorder, because they're not people you're comfortable discussing it with. And you may have friends you're very comfortable with and with whom you can share a lot of information. This activity will help you think about the people you can rely on to help you with your bipolar disorder and how they can do that.

for you to do

Picture yourself in the inner circle. Around "ME," write the names of the people you are most comfortable sharing information with.

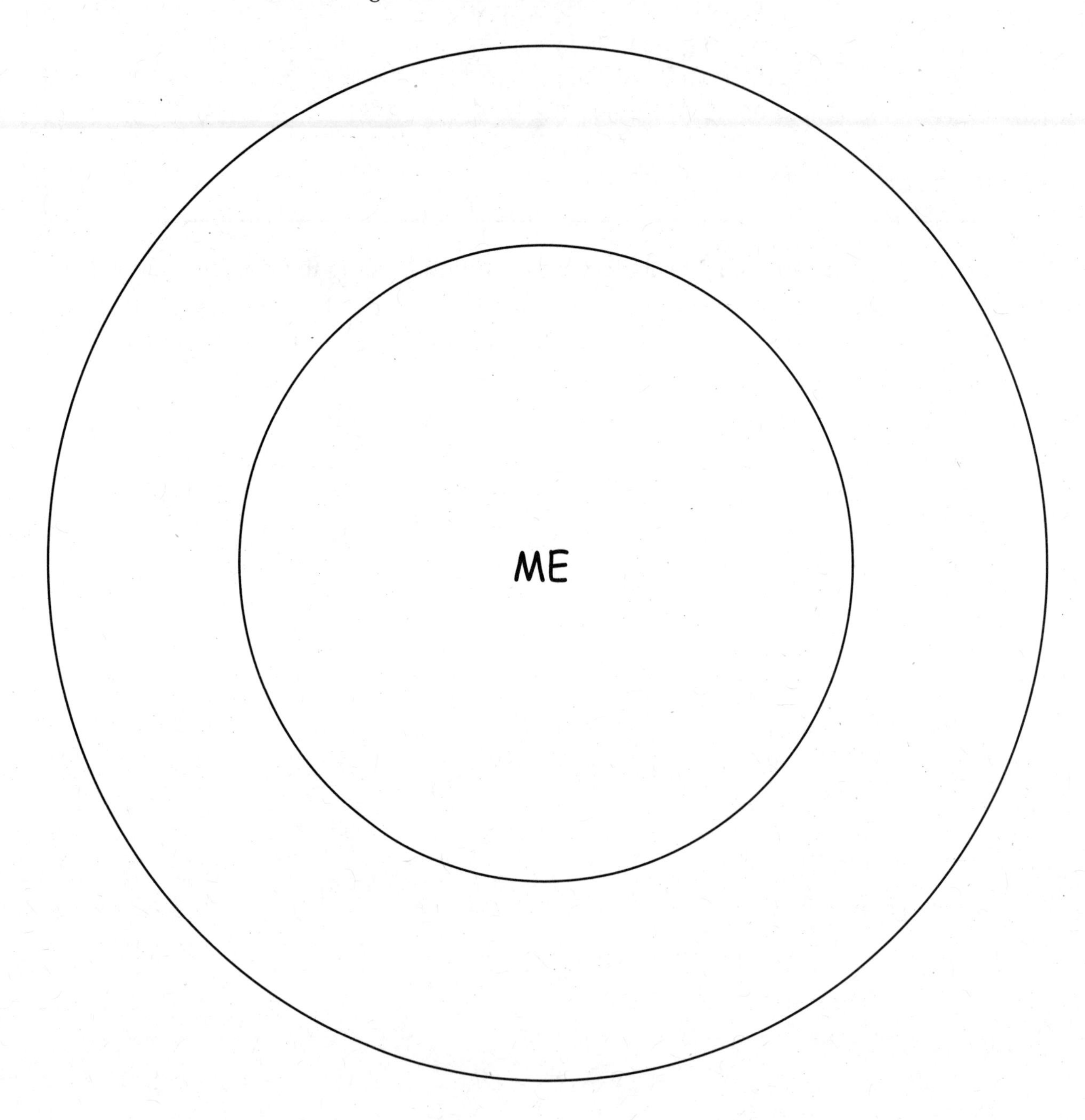

In the outer circle, write the names of people you might share some information with but are not as close or comfortable with as your inner circle. These people might be a favorite teacher or guidance counselor, friends you're not quite as close with, people you work with, extended-family members, and so on.

Outside the circle, you can put the names of some people with whom you would not want to share anything about your condition even if they're supportive of you in other ways, like people you chat with on Facebook.

Now that you have a more concrete picture, you can start to think about how these people can best help you. You're not likely to ask the people outside the circle for help, since you're not comfortable sharing information with them about your bipolar disorder. So we're going to concentrate on the people inside the circles, starting with the inner circle—those closest to you. These are the people who know that you have bipolar disorder, and you'll have shared at least some of your emotions and experiences with them, so they understand in part what it means for your life.

How could they help you? We've started you off with some examples:

- My parents could remind me to take my medications.
- My sister could stop herself from teasing me when I'm already feeling depressed.
- My best friend could call to say hi, even when I don't return her calls.
- ______________________________
- ______________________________
- ______________________________
- ______________________________
- ______________________________
- ______________________________

Now think about how the people in your outer circle can help. Remember, what you ask of people is going to depend on how much information you're comfortable giving them.

- My guidance counselor can provide a quiet place for me when my mood starts to get high at school.
- My employer can schedule my hours so that I don't have midnight shifts.
- My friend Linda, who knows I have anxiety problems, can talk to me when I'm getting anxious in class.
- ______________________________
- ______________________________
- ______________________________
- ______________________________
- ______________________________
- ______________________________

… and more to do

The things people do to try to help you may sometimes just trigger more emotions in you. For example, maybe your parents constantly ask if you remembered to take your medications, which makes you angry; or maybe it feels like your family walks on eggshells around you to avoid upsetting you, which makes you feel lonely. Write down some of the ways people try to help, but which you don't find helpful:

____

____

____

____

____

____

Remember, your friends and family who know about your bipolar disorder more than likely want to help you. Sometimes they don't know how to help, so you need to tell them.

Once you've completed these lists, your next task is to begin asking people for help. The more people you have supporting you in your life, the stronger you'll be. If you have problems talking to your family and friends, turn to Activities 33 and 34 for some tips on communication.

5 how living in the present moment can help

for you to know

Many of us spend a lot of time living in the past or the future rather than truly living in the present. Mindfulness means intentionally focusing on one thing at a time with your full attention, in the present moment, and without judgment. It helps you notice what your mind is doing and what feelings you are having. You can then choose whether to stay with these thoughts and feelings or let them go.

Amir was great at multitasking. He could study for a test, chat on Facebook, and listen to music at the same time. While he noticed that it took him longer to finish studying, he didn't mind because at least he was enjoying himself.

But when Amir was diagnosed with bipolar disorder, there were more serious consequences to his multitasking: by not paying attention to his present experience, he might miss some really important clues that signaled the start of a manic or depressive episode. Amir needed to learn to recognize what triggered his episodes and what their symptoms were so that he could better manage his condition. His relationship with himself needed to change so that he could act as his own coach, monitoring himself more closely. To do this, he had to pay attention to his experiences in the present moment; he needed to practice mindfulness.

for you to do

For the next sixty seconds, focus your attention on the picture below. Then answer the following questions.

What did you notice about your attention as you were trying to stay focused on the picture? Was it easy for you to stay focused? Or were you aware that your mind began to drift to other things?

What thoughts, memories, images, or feelings came to you as you tried to focus only on the picture? Write them in the space provided.

If your attention drifted, did you judge yourself (for example, by saying, "Wow, I can't even do this right")? Or did you simply accept that this happened and bring your attention back to the picture ("Oops, I'm not focusing. Let's go back to the picture")?

... and more to do

If you learned to be mindful—to notice and accept your experiences, including your thoughts and feelings—how might it help you? Add your own responses to these examples.

- I might become more comfortable with my feelings and not try to push them away.
- I might feel calmer.
- ____
- ____
- ____
- ____

How might mindfulness help you manage your bipolar disorder?

- I might notice negative thinking and be able to take steps to help myself feel better.
- I might notice signs that I am heading toward a manic or depressive episode.
- ____
- ____
- ____
- ____

If you are having a hard time thinking about this, ask someone you trust for ideas.

automatic behaviors and their impact

6

for you to know

We often do things without being aware that we are doing them. Our minds are like busy bees, darting from thought to thought. For example, when you eat, you might also watch television, surf the net, talk to others, listen to music, or read. How many times have you eaten more than you wanted or barely remembered how the food tasted? When your mind is thinking about something else, you aren't as aware of what you are doing in the present moment. This can waste a lot of time and energy, and it makes you less likely to make helpful choices.

Amir had a lot of difficulty remembering to take his medication, partly because he had a lot on his mind. In the morning, he was busy thinking about catching the bus and what might happen that day. In the evening, he was busy thinking about all of the homework he had to do and about how the day had gone. He would often forget to take his medication altogether or think he had taken it when he really hadn't. Sometimes he would accidentally take it twice because he forgot he had already taken it.

A large part of Amir's problem with taking his medication was that he was on automatic pilot much of the time: he could brush his teeth, shower, and eat breakfast while thinking about what the day would bring rather than concentrating on the activity he was doing. Does this sound familiar?

for you to do

Here are some behaviors that people often do mindlessly. What are some things you do without really paying attention to them?

- walking
- listening to a friend
- doing homework
- using the computer
- ______________________________
- ______________________________
- ______________________________
- ______________________________

What are the possible consequences of not paying attention to what you're doing? Some common ones are listed below.

- You make more mistakes.
- You waste time and energy.
- You find scrapes or other injuries on your body and don't know how they got there.
- You get caught up in painful thoughts and emotions.
- ______________________________
- ______________________________
- ______________________________
- ______________________________

What are some activities you already do that are easy for you to fully focus your attention on?

- playing guitar
- reading a great book
- ______________________
- ______________________
- playing with a pet
- watching a favorite tv show
- ______________________
- ______________________

Write what you notice about your experience during these times. For example, what thoughts go through your mind while you are doing the activity? How do you feel during and after the activity?

____

____

____

Do you experience these activities differently when you are more accepting compared to when you are less accepting (for example, by judging your performance or events of the day)?

____

____

____

... and more to do

Thinking about the exercise you've just completed, write some thoughts about mindfulness and how it relates to you. For example, do you need to work on spending more time in the present and less time in the past or future? Perhaps you notice you're often on automatic pilot and need to work on doing more things with awareness. Or maybe you notice you tend to judge a lot and could benefit from working on acceptance. Write about what you would like to work on in order to be more mindful.

____

____

____

____

____

____

____

____

____

informal activities to practice mindfully 7

for you to know

Learning to notice and accept your thoughts and feelings can help you manage stress more effectively, quiet your worries, and feel calmer. Mindfulness can also help you be more effective in your life, for example, by helping you notice symptoms that may be clues to the start of a depressive or manic episode. You don't have to set aside special time to practice mindfulness; at least once a day, try to make it part of activities you already do.

Amir began his own process of developing mindfulness by trying to closely listen to songs on his MP3 player. This was difficult for him because listening to music usually reminded him of something from his past, such as his first relationship. He still had a difficult time accepting these past events and would feel very sad.

Does this kind of thing ever happen to you?

for you to do

The next time you listen to a song on the radio or on your MP3 player, notice whether you are focusing on the song or getting caught up in the thoughts, images, memories, or feelings it brings up for you. Write what you notice below. For example, did you notice your attention drifting away? If so, what were the thoughts and feelings that your attention drifted to? Were you able to gently invite your attention back to the song? Were you able to do this without judging yourself?

____

____

____

Now, listen to the same song again. Pick one aspect of the music to follow. It may be the sound of the singer's voice, the lyrics, or one of the instruments. Also pay attention to any feelings you experience as you listen. When you notice your attention drifting to something else, gently invite it back to the song. You will have to do this many times, possibly hundreds, so don't be hard on yourself! Write about your experience below.

____

____

____

Compare these two experiences in terms of how you felt.

Feelings I noticed while listening mindfully:	**Feelings I noticed while listening mindlessly:**
__________________________	__________________________
__________________________	__________________________
__________________________	__________________________

... and more to do

You can do *everything* mindfully. Choose what you're going to be mindful of (like speaking with a friend, listening to your MP3 player, doing your homework, skateboarding). Begin to focus on that activity and, without judging yourself, bring your attention back to the activity when your mind wanders. Mindfulness can be challenging, so be gentle with yourself if you have difficulties with it.

8 formal activities to practice mindfully

for you to know

In addition to making mindfulness part of your everyday activities, you can also practice it more formally. You may find that setting aside time each day to practice mindfulness and using a more structured activity is more helpful to you.

Amir tried formal mindfulness practices as well. He started by learning to pay attention to his breath. Every evening before he began his homework, he would turn off his phone and music and then begin his breathing exercise.

At first, he found himself thinking that it was more trouble than it was worth. He told himself that he would never be good at it and thought, "What's the point?" Then he noticed that he was constantly evaluating how well he was doing. When he stopped judging himself so much, he felt more motivated and hopeful about it.

for you to do

Sit in a comfortable position, with your back straight, feet on the floor, hands on your lap. Now pay attention to the rise and fall of your stomach as you inhale and exhale. When you breathe in, count one; when you breathe out, count two; in three; out four. Count up to ten and then start back at one again. When you notice your mind wandering (which it will, and probably many times!), just bring your attention back to your breath and start counting at the number "one."

Remember, the goal here isn't to stop the thoughts from coming—the job of your brain is to generate thoughts, so it's nearly impossible to stop them. Instead, just *notice without judgment* that your attention has drifted away from your breath and invite your attention back to the present moment. You can also do this exercise lying down; it can sometimes help you to fall asleep at night.

After you have tried this exercise, write about your experience with it. Did you notice your attention drifting? What were the thoughts and feelings that your attention drifted to? Were you able to gently bring your attention back to your breathing or did you judge yourself in some way? Write about what you noticed:

____

____

____

____

____

____

____

____

... and more to do

What thoughts, feelings, and beliefs do you have about your ability to practice mindfulness?

____

____

How do these affect your willingness to practice? Do they make you feel frustrated and lead to self-doubt? Or do they help you feel more confident and motivated about practicing?

____

____

What other experiences do you have with learning new things (for example, learning how to skateboard or learning Spanish in school)?

____

____

What skills and qualities helped you in these learning experiences? We've listed some possibilities to get you started:

- patience
- focus
- ______________________
- ______________________
- hopefulness
- trust in yourself
- ______________________
- ______________________

How will these skills and qualities be useful to you in learning this new skill of mindfulness?

____

____

The goal is to live your life more mindfully, so start practicing mindfulness daily. You can use the following log to record your experiences: write down the date, what you did mindfully, and how long you did it for. In the final column, make any notes about your experience: whether it was difficult or not, whether you were easily distracted or very focused, where your thoughts wandered to, and so on. We've given you some examples.

Date	What I Did Mindfully	How Long I Practiced	What I Noticed
Aug. 10	Listened to my MP3 player and paid attention to one of the instruments	2 minutes	I was feeling sad because the song reminded me of my ex. Tried to stay in the present moment, but it was hard.
Aug. 11	Breathing	5 minutes	Less distracted today. I was able to keep bringing my attention back to my breathing. It was calming.
Aug. 12	Eating a cookie	1 minute	It tasted so good! I could really feel the soft texture on my tongue and I noticed how different the chocolate chips felt compared to the rest of it.
Aug. 13	Breathing	2 minutes	Much more difficult today. I noticed that my thoughts were racing and I was feeling quite anxious but I kept bringing my attention back to my breath.

Date	What I Did Mindfully	How Long I Practiced	What I Noticed

your emotional self versus your wise self 9

for you to know

We all have times when our emotions overwhelm us and have a big effect on our actions. For example, when you're feeling really depressed, you may hide away from other people. When you're feeling manic, you are probably more social and outgoing and look for activities to do. And if you have a crush on someone, you might do some crazy things you wouldn't normally do! Dialectical behavior therapy (DBT) calls this thinking with your ***emotion mind***, and in this workbook, we refer to it as thinking with your ***emotional self***. When you think logically before acting, you are using your ***wise mind*** (according to DBT), or your ***wise self***.

When Kyle felt depressed, he would spend a lot of time in his bedroom, coming out only when he had to (like to eat) and sleeping a lot. He also felt really angry when he was depressed and he often took his anger out on his family for trying to help him: he would yell at them to just leave him alone. Kyle's emotional self was controlling how he was acting.

While it's very important to let yourself feel your feelings, if you're reacting—acting based only on your emotions—you might act in ways that aren't in your best interest, which can get you into trouble. The trick is to consider how you feel about something, and at the same time let your wise self think logically about a situation before deciding what do.

When Christina became depressed, she would have a hard time getting out of bed in the morning and would often skip her morning classes. When her grades began to drop, she realized she had to stop doing this. So one morning, she woke up feeling pretty miserable and, even though her first thought was that she couldn't get out of bed, she reminded herself why she needed to get to school and forced herself to go in spite of her mood. Christina's wise self was controlling her actions.

for you to do

In each of these situation, first tell how you might react with your emotional self. Then write about how you might choose to act from your wise self.

Emotional reaction: ______________________

____

____

Wise reaction: ___________________________

____

____

Emotional reaction: ______________________

____

____

Wise reaction: ___________________________

____

____

Emotional reaction: ______________________

____

____

Wise reaction: ___________________________

____

____

... and more to do

Tell about times when you acted from your emotional self.

When your emotions were controlling your behavior, how did you feel later? Did you feel good about your behavior? Did you feel embarrassed or ashamed, or have other negative emotions about how you acted?

Did you feel as though this behavior helped you work toward your goals in life or made it harder?

Tell about some times when you've acted from your wise self.

Think about times when you had really strong emotions but prevented them from controlling your behavior. How did you manage to do that?

10 how to increase your wise-self behavior

for you to know

Certain things you do might make it more likely that you'll be acting from your emotional self. But just as wisdom is a balancing of emotions and logical thinking, you can learn to balance different areas of your life in order to reduce the amount of time you spend in your emotional self and get to your wise self more often.

When he's feeling good, Carm goes to classes regularly. He plays basketball after school, is active in the Spanish Club, and enjoys writing short stories and poetry. He also works part-time at a video store. He likes his job and the people he works with and he is saving his money to go on a trip to Florida with his friends next spring.

When his mood starts to get low, Carm sleeps more. He takes a nap in the afternoon when he gets home from school, which means he usually skips basketball and Spanish Club. He sometimes calls in sick to work because he can't be bothered going and he stops doing other things he enjoys, like writing. He also doesn't eat as much because his appetite disappears.

When Carm acts on the urge to withdraw from his usual activities and to change his sleeping and eating patterns, it makes it more likely that his emotional self will take over.

Withdrawing from others, sleeping too much, and not eating properly are all examples of things that make people more emotional—and when you have bipolar disorder, these things make it more likely you'll have symptoms.

You may also experience changes like these, and it's important to remember that many of these can bring on or worsen your bipolar symptoms. By continuing to take care of yourself, you can help yourself feel better emotionally.

for you to do

Use these spaces to illustrate how your behaviors and emotions change when you are depressed, and when you're in a manic or mixed episode. You can draw images or you can cut pictures out from old magazines or newspapers, if you prefer.

When you start to experience symptoms of bipolar disorder, what changes do you make in your life that probably aren't helpful? This could include sleeping more or less, stopping regular activities that you enjoy, no longer exercising, isolating yourself from others, not eating in a balanced way, and so on.

1. ______________________________

2. ______________________________

3. ______________________________

4. ______________________________

5. ______________________________

Look at each of these changes in turn and think about what you can do differently to help you get back to yourself:

1. ______________________________

2. ______________________________

3. ______________________________

4. ______________________________

5. ______________________________

It's important to set small goals for yourself to get you started in the direction you want to go. If you make these goals realistic, it's more likely you'll reach them. If you make goals too big, they're more difficult to reach and you might end up feeling bad about yourself for not doing what you set out to do.

Choose one of the changes you'd like to make and write it here (for example, "I need to stop sleeping so much"):

____

Write down one small, realistic step you can take in that direction (for example, "I will set my alarm for fifteen minutes earlier tomorrow morning" or "I will go to bed fifteen minutes later tonight"):

____

Start by taking that one small step and don't forget to congratulate yourself—making these kinds of changes is usually quite difficult! Then think about the next steps you need to take to reach your goal and write them here (for example, your next step to decrease sleep might be to set your alarm for another fifteen minutes earlier or to nap for only one hour instead of one-and-a-half hours):

- ______________________________________
- ______________________________________
- ______________________________________
- ______________________________________
- ______________________________________
- ______________________________________
- ______________________________________

… and more to do

When your emotions are troubling you, it often feels easier to just stop trying. You might stop going to school, doing extracurricular activities, going to work, and even just getting out of bed in the morning. But by giving up these things, you stop experiencing those accomplishments that make you feel good about yourself, and that can leave you feeling worse.

List some activities that give you a sense of accomplishment and make you feel good about yourself (for example, getting out of bed in the morning, doing volunteer work, getting a good grade, going out with friends, responding to e-mail):

- ______________________
- ______________________
- ______________________
- ______________________
- ______________________
- ______________________
- ______________________
- ______________________

What other things might give you this same feeling of accomplishment or success?

____

____

If you haven't been doing any of these things recently, what's one thing you could do today?

____

Over the coming weeks, you'll need to work on these goals, but trying to reach all of them at once might be overwhelming. So start with one and when you've reached that goal, move on to the next one. Make sure you pat yourself on the back when you're moving in the right direction, even if you don't completely meet your goal. Be kind to yourself!

keeping track of your mood 11

for you to know

It can be really helpful for you to keep track of your mood from day to day so that you'll notice when your mood starts to become depressed, manic, or mixed. Keeping track of your mood can also help you know if any of the changes you're making are having the effect of increasing the amount of time you're spending in your wise self.

Staying well sometimes takes a lot of hard work. The good news is, the tools are all here to help take you care of yourself and prevent, or at least limit, future depressive and manic episodes. The mood chart is one tool that is really important in helping you do this.

for you to do

The following chart can help you keep track, on a daily basis, of your mood as well as some of the factors that can influence how you're feeling. Make several copies of the chart. Each day, circle the number that best reflects your mood and energy level. Fill in the number of hours you slept the night before, circle YES or NO to indicate whether you took your medication that day, and use the blank lines to add some brief notes about any positive or negative events that might have affected your mood.

Mood Chart: Week of ________________________

Monday Circle the highest you felt and the lowest you felt today.

Mood	1 Really sad	2	3	4	5 Neutral	6	7	8	9	10 Very happy
Energy	1 Tired	2	3	4	5 Neutral	6	7	8	9	10 Hyper

Hours of sleep last night: ________ I took my meds today: YES NO

Negative or positive events that happened today: ________________________

Tuesday Circle the highest you felt and the lowest you felt today.

Mood	1 Really sad	2	3	4	5 Neutral	6	7	8	9	10 Very happy
Energy	1 Tired	2	3	4	5 Neutral	6	7	8	9	10 Hyper

Hours of sleep last night: ________ I took my meds today: YES NO

Negative or positive events that happened today: ________________________

Wednesday Circle the highest you felt and the lowest you felt today.

Mood	1 Really sad	2	3	4	5 Neutral	6	7	8	9	10 Very happy
Energy	1 Tired	2	3	4	5 Neutral	6	7	8	9	10 Hyper

Hours of sleep last night: ________ I took my meds today: YES NO

Negative or positive events that happened today: ________________________

Thursday Circle the highest you felt and the lowest you felt today.

Mood	☹	1 Really sad	2	3	4	5 Neutral	6	7	8	9	10 Very happy ☺
Energy	☹	1 Tired	2	3	4	5 Neutral	6	7	8	9	10 Hyper ☺

Hours of sleep last night: ________ I took my meds today: YES NO

Negative or positive events that happened today: ______________________________

Friday Circle the highest you felt and the lowest you felt today.

Mood	☹	1 Really sad	2	3	4	5 Neutral	6	7	8	9	10 Very happy ☺
Energy	☹	1 Tired	2	3	4	5 Neutral	6	7	8	9	10 Hyper ☺

Hours of sleep last night: ________ I took my meds today: YES NO

Negative or positive events that happened today: ______________________________

Saturday Circle the highest you felt and the lowest you felt today.

Mood	☹	1 Really sad	2	3	4	5 Neutral	6	7	8	9	10 Very happy ☺
Energy	☹	1 Tired	2	3	4	5 Neutral	6	7	8	9	10 Hyper ☺

Hours of sleep last night: ________ I took my meds today: YES NO

Negative or positive events that happened today: ______________________________

Sunday Circle the highest you felt and the lowest you felt today.

Mood	☹	1 Really sad	2	3	4	5 Neutral	6	7	8	9	10 Very happy ☺
Energy	☹	1 Tired	2	3	4	5 Neutral	6	7	8	9	10 Hyper ☺

Hours of sleep last night: ________ I took my meds today: YES NO

Negative or positive events that happened today: ______________________________

... and more to do

As you continue to do these mood charts, you might see some patterns emerge—for example, that when you don't get enough sleep, or if you sleep too much, your mood is affected. A mood chart also helps you to see symptoms as they start to happen, giving you advance warning when a new episode might be emerging.

how to identify your emotions 12

for you to know

People often find themselves unable to identify what emotion they're feeling: they may realize that they feel "bad" or "upset," but they can't put a specific name on the emotion. If you don't know what emotion you feel, it's hard to figure out what you can do about it.

Do you usually have a hard time identifying your emotions? Are you able to name your feelings as you experience them or do you find that you get lost in the "emotional fog," where you know you feel something, but it's unclear to you what the feeling is?

Learning more about how you experience your emotions will help you manage them more effectively. In the long run, this means you'll be more able to act from your wise self, rather than reacting from your emotional self.

It is also important for you to learn the difference between emotional states that come from your bipolar disorder and those that you would feel anyway. For instance, everyone gets sad sometimes; when you have bipolar disorder, your challenge is to distinguish between feeling sad and entering a state of bipolar depression. Likewise, everyone gets hyper or excited at times; you'll need to learn what this typical emotion feels like versus what it feels like to enter a manic episode.

for you to do

Emotions generally fall into one of four categories: angry, sad, happy, and scared. See if you can place each emotion listed below into the most accurate category.

Angry	Sad	Happy	Scared
____________	____________	____________	____________
____________	____________	____________	____________
____________	____________	____________	____________
____________	____________	____________	____________
____________	____________	____________	____________
____________	____________	____________	____________
____________	____________	____________	____________
____________	____________	____________	____________
____________	____________	____________	____________

mad	depressed	blue	stressed
anxious	alarmed	ecstatic	apprehensive
relaxed	thrilled	nervous	worried
annoyed	frustrated	afraid	concerned
peaceful	panicky	glum	relieved
down	resentful	hurt	overjoyed
comfortable	excited	fulfilled	sorrowful
irritated	enraged	furious	grieving
bitter	heartbroken	pained	lonely

... and more to do

Once you're more familiar with your emotions and can name what you're feeling, it's important for you to notice how you feel about your feelings.

Look back at the earlier list of emotions and use a blue pen or marker to circle the feelings you don't mind having: you might not enjoy the feeling but you can accept that you have it without feeling anxious. Next, use a red pen or marker to circle the emotions you don't like having and that you try to avoid or push away.

Over the next couple of weeks, notice how you feel about your feelings and any thoughts you have about these feelings. Make any notes about what you notice in the space provided.

Angry: ______________________________

____

Sad: ______________________________

____

Happy: ______________________________

____

Scared: ______________________________

____

13 the physical part of emotions

for you to know

Feelings are made up of a lot more than just the way we feel; they also include physical sensations, thoughts, and urges. Emotions impact people differently, and it's important for you to get to know your own emotions so that you can manage them more effectively.

Bella's grandmother died quite suddenly when Bella was in her last year of high school. She had been quite close to her grandmother, and after her death, Bella knew she wasn't feeling like herself. Every day, she woke up with a stomachache that lasted most of the morning. She didn't want to see her friends and was skipping her favorite activities: playing volleyball after school and coaching the junior basketball team. She was irritable and would snap at people for the smallest reason, so she thought she was angry, or perhaps starting to experience a depressive episode.

One day, when she was talking to her best friend, Sarah, about the loss of her grandmother, Bella started to cry and couldn't stop. Sarah pointed out that Bella had lost someone who was incredibly important in her life and that she must miss her grandmother a lot. Bella began to realize that she wasn't angry or depressed at all; she was lonely and still grieving.

Once Bella figured this out, her emotions didn't go away, but she was more able to manage them and to prevent herself from lashing out at other people. Being able to identify the emotion meant that Bella was able to identify the problem that had triggered the emotion. This, in turn, meant that she could work on solving that problem (in this case, by allowing herself to grieve) in order to help alleviate the pain.

for you to do

Imagine that each body represents yours. On each picture, show where in your body you feel that emotion. For example, if you feel the blood rush to your face when you become angry, you might color the face red. If you cry, like Bella, when you feel sad, you might put tears on the face of the sad body. If it is hard for you to identify the physical sensations you experience, notice what happens the next time you feel these emotions, and then come back to this exercise.

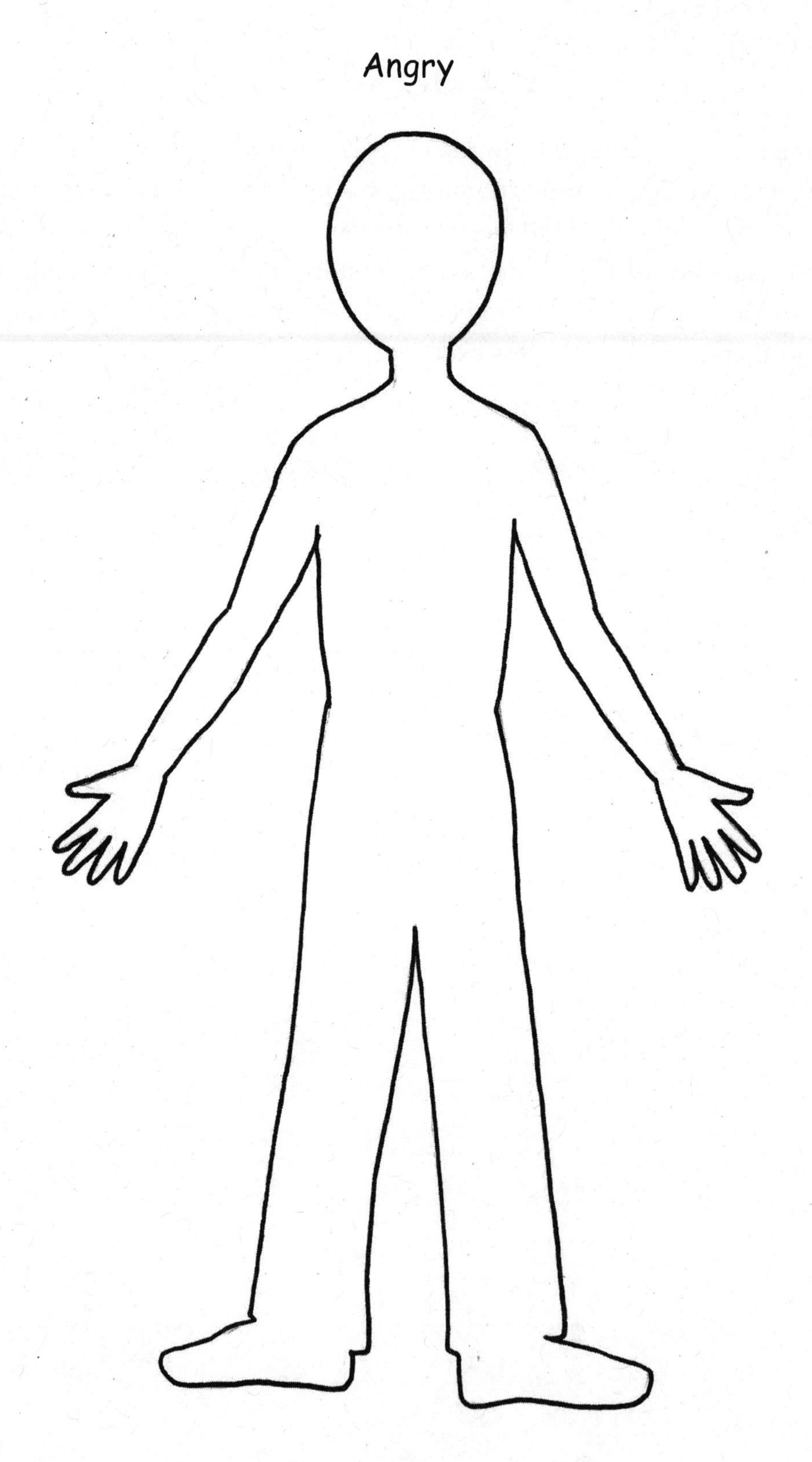
Angry

Sad

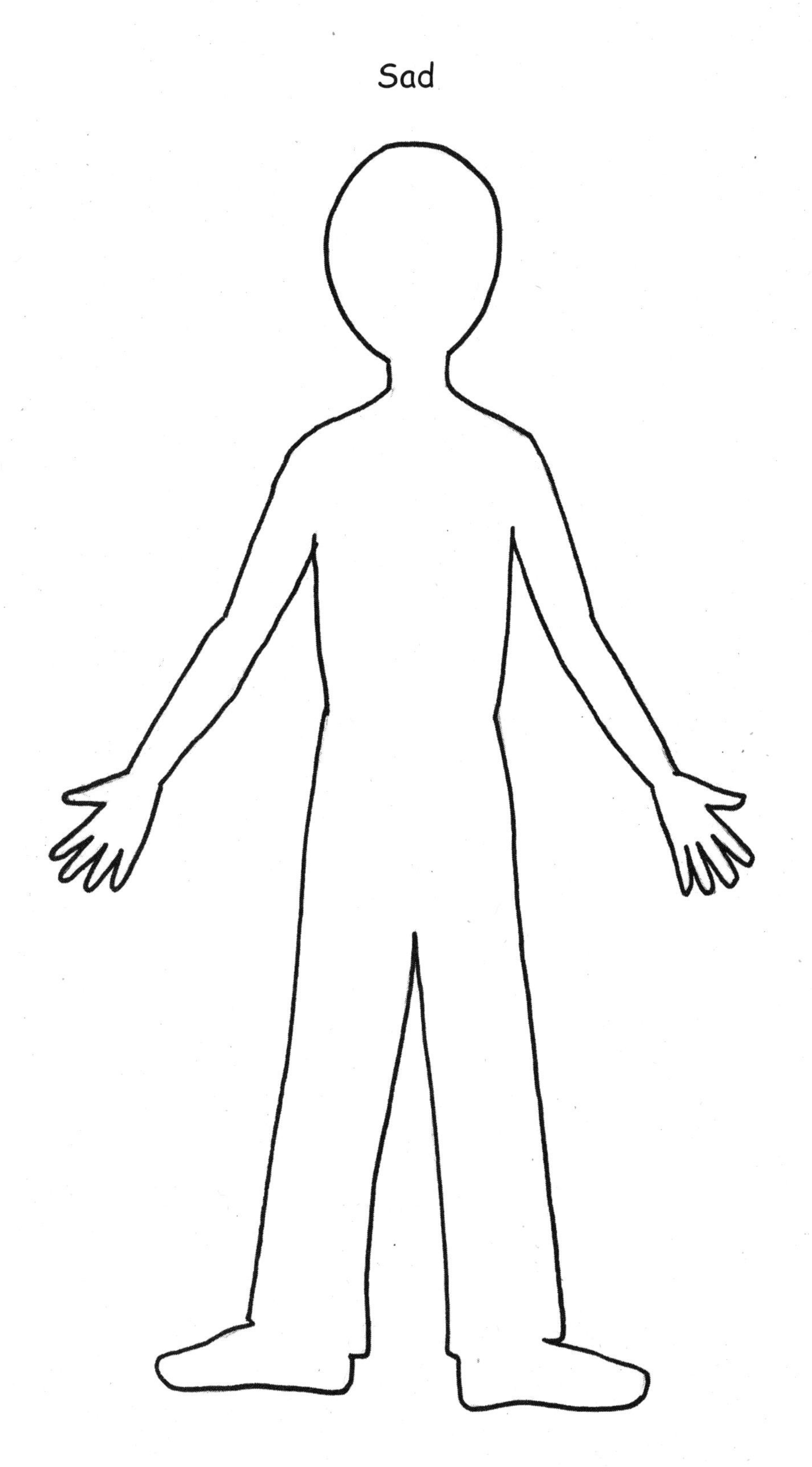

Happy

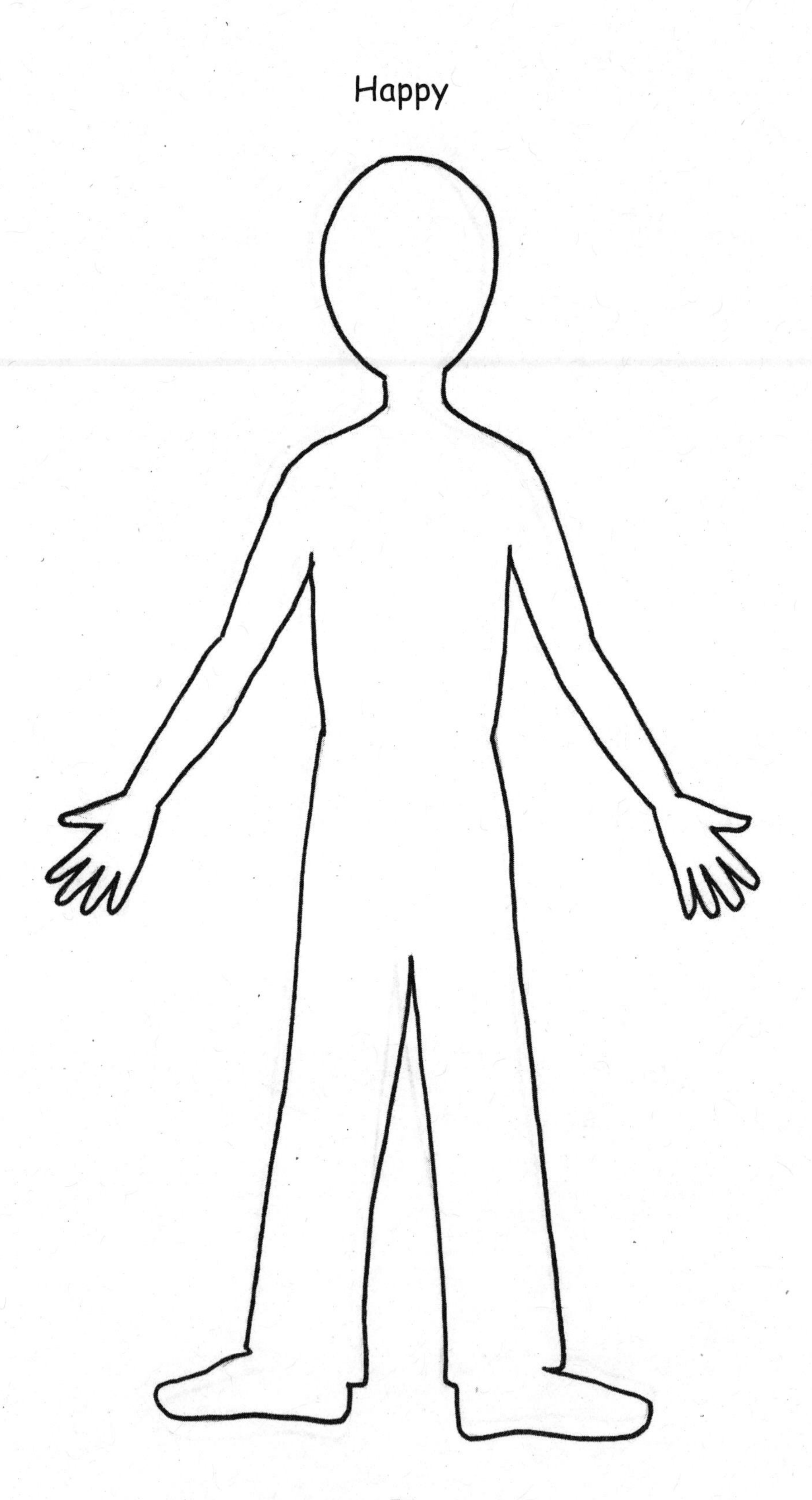

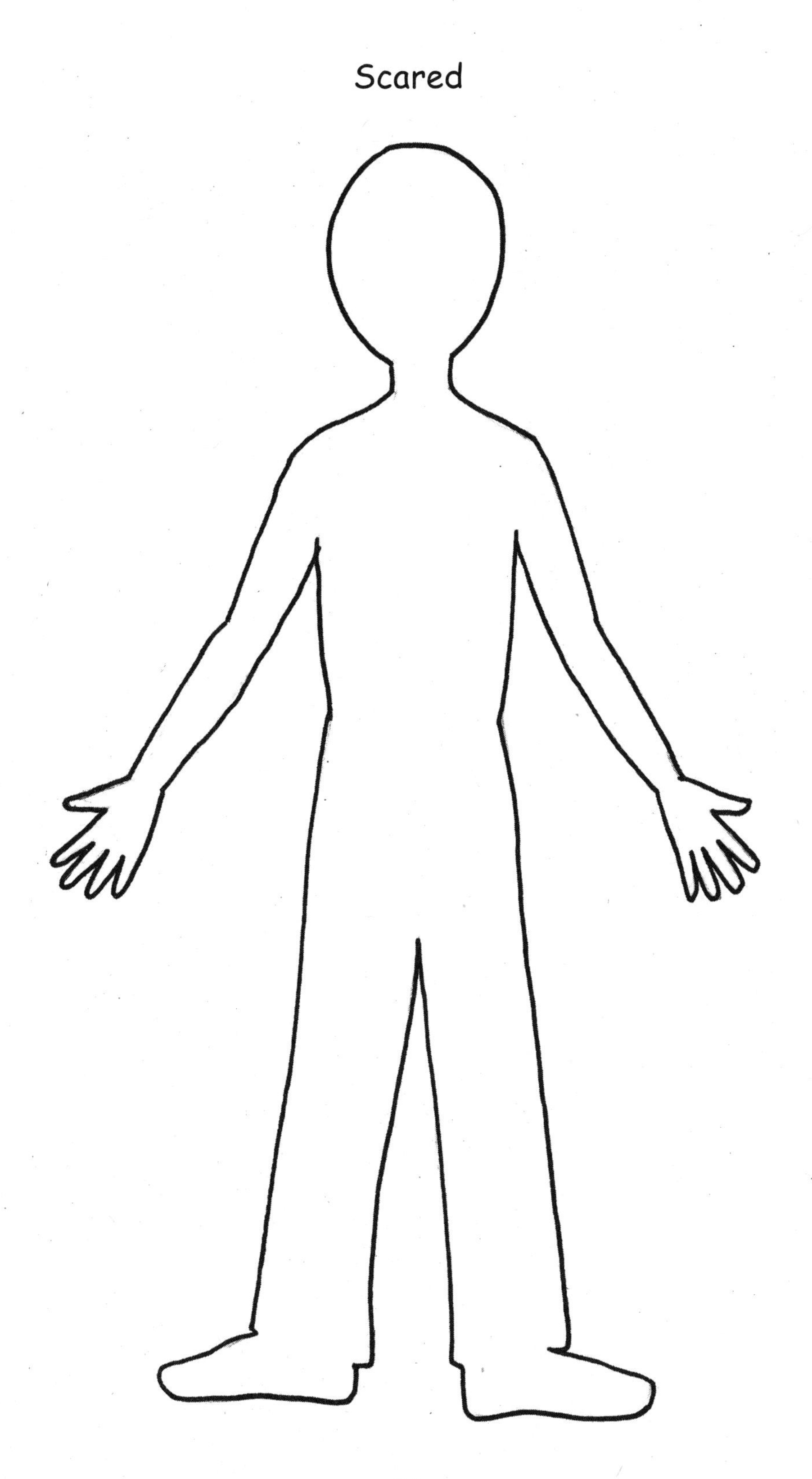
Scared

… and more to do

The physical sensations that come with an emotion often trigger thoughts that further affect how you feel. For example, when you get anxious, your heart might start to beat really quickly, which can lead to thoughts of having a heart attack. This, in turn, can make you feel even more scared. Or you might feel angry and then think something like, "I shouldn't feel this way; it's wrong," which might cause you to also feel guilt, or anger at yourself.

Looking at each of the bodies above, try to identify some thoughts that you have about the physical sensations you experience. Then, see if you can relate each thought to an additional feeling you might have, and fill in the following chart.

Initial Emotion	Thoughts About Sensations	Additional Feelings
Angry		
Sad		
Happy		
Scared		

thoughts, feelings, and behaviors 14

for you to know

When emotions are really intense, it can be difficult to tell the difference between thoughts, feelings, and behaviors. Being able to tell the difference between these three things can help you act from your wise self.

Sydney would go through periods where she felt "bad" or "upset," but she often wasn't able to figure out specifically what emotion she was having or why she was feeling that way. It seemed like her emotions were just one big tangled mess, and so she usually didn't know what to do about them. Once Sydney learned how to separate her emotional experience into thoughts, feelings, and behaviors, she found that she had more control over each of these things. For example, she learned to tell the difference between feeling depressed and feeling sad, and realized that depression was part of her bipolar, whereas sadness is an emotion everyone feels at times. With this additional knowledge and the control it gave her, she was able to decrease the intensity of her emotions.

for you to do

For each of the following statements, indicate, by circling the most accurate word, whether a thought, feeling, or behavior is being described.

1. During an argument with your best friend, you throw your cell phone at the wall.

   Thought Feeling Behavior

2. You'd like to quit school.

   Thought Feeling Behavior

3. You're angry because you have bipolar disorder.

   Thought Feeling Behavior

4. You're chatting on Facebook.

   Thought Feeling Behavior

5. You're nervous about a math test coming up.

   Thought Feeling Behavior

6. You don't want to take your medication because it makes you tired.

   Thought Feeling Behavior

7. You're sad because the person you like has a girlfriend or boyfriend.

   Thought Feeling Behavior

8. You go to the movies with your friends.

   Thought Feeling Behavior

9. You're angry because you got detention for goofing around in class.

   Thought Feeling Behavior

10. You want people to like you.

    Thought Feeling Behavior

Answers: 1. behavior; 2. thought; 3. feeling; 4. behavior; 5. feeling; 6 thought; 7. feeling; 8. behavior; 9. feeling; 10. thought

... and more to do

Compare your answers to the correct responses. Did you have a hard time telling the difference between thoughts, feelings, and behaviors? Explain your answer.

___

___

___

___

Do you think that you have a hard time telling the difference between your own thoughts, feelings, and behaviors? Explain your answer.

___

___

___

___

Learning to tell the difference between these three things is one of the keys to managing your emotions and behaving in more effective ways. Over the next few days, practice noticing how you feel, what your thoughts are, and what your behavior is. You can do this by purposely listing these things off to yourself in your head. For example, "I feel content, I'm thinking about how much I love my dog, and I'm sitting here petting her."

15 emotions and urges

for you to know

An urge is the combination of thoughts and feelings that make you feel like you want to do something. Usually when you're acting on an urge, you're acting from your emotional self, which is often not in your best interest. Just because you have an urge, doesn't mean you have to act on it!

How many times have you had a strong emotional reaction and simply acted without really taking time to think about what you're doing? For example, when you're feeling angry, you lash out at someone and say something hurtful. Or, like Bella in Activity 13, your negative feelings lead you to isolate yourself and withdraw from things you previously enjoyed. Generally, when you're acting from your emotional self, you're acting on an urge rather than choosing how to act in a situation in spite of your feelings.

for you to do

For each picture below, think about what emotion the person seems to be feeling, and tell what urges might come up for that person.

... and more to do

Think about some times when you've felt these emotions and write down the urges that you experienced with each.

	Situation	Urge
Angry:	____________________	____________________
	____________________	____________________
	____________________	____________________
Sad:	____________________	____________________
	____________________	____________________
	____________________	____________________
Happy:	____________________	____________________
	____________________	____________________
	____________________	____________________
Scared:	____________________	____________________
	____________________	____________________
	____________________	____________________

When you have an urge, you can actually change the emotion you're feeling by doing something opposite to what you feel like doing. If you feel angry at someone, and your urge is to strike out (for example, by yelling or throwing something), see if you can do the opposite: just avoid that person instead of confronting him or her. When you're scared, often the urge is to avoid whatever's causing the anxiety. Instead, try approaching the situation; doing that can help decrease the anxiety.

Look at the urges you wrote down and see if you can come up with an opposite action for each of them.

	Urge	Opposite Action
Angry:	__________	__________
	__________	__________
	__________	__________
Sad:	__________	__________
	__________	__________
	__________	__________
Happy:	__________	__________
	__________	__________
	__________	__________
Scared:	__________	__________
	__________	__________
	__________	__________

The next time you're feeling an intense emotion and you have an urge to act from your emotional self, see if you can do the opposite. Then write about what happened.

____

____

____

____

____

16 dealing with intense emotions

for you to know

Everybody has times of crisis when emotions get really intense and are hard to deal with. When that happens to you, you may have urges to do things that might help you cope with the overwhelming feelings in the short run but that also have negative consequences for you.

Trina was already feeling depressed when her boyfriend, Jim, texted to cancel the plans they had made for that night. She was so angry, hurt, and disappointed that she didn't even text back. She had been looking forward to spending time with Jim, so when he cancelled it felt like more than she could bear. Soon after, Trina began to have thoughts about Jim not really caring about her, and these thoughts led to feelings of worthlessness and even more intense sadness. Wanting to escape this emotional pain, Trina impulsively swallowed a handful of her medication.

Have you ever had feelings so intense that you just didn't know how to cope with them? This can happen in all sorts of situations: for example, when you are in a depression or mania; when someone you care about dies; when you have an argument with a friend; when you get a poor grade in school; when you're feeling anxious and overwhelmed with all the work you have to do.

No matter what the situation, in trying to cope with the intense feelings that result, you might engage in some kind of behavior that just ends up making the situation worse—whether it's overdosing like Trina, hurting yourself in some way (for example, by cutting or burning yourself), using drugs or alcohol, and so on.

for you to do

In the space below, list what you've done to cope in situations where you experienced intense feelings. Then check off whether each was

- a helpful behavior (like talking to someone you trust);
- a neutral behavior, which might not help, but doesn't usually make things worse (like sleeping);
- an unhelpful behavior that made the situation worse by having a negative impact on you or others (like using substances or isolating yourself).

If you're not sure if a behavior was helpful or not, think about its aftereffects: Did the behavior make the situation better or worse for you? In the long run, did it have negative consequences? If you're still not sure, you may want to ask someone you trust for their opinion.

What You Did to Cope:	Helpful	Neutral	Unhelpful
______________________________	______	______	______
______________________________	______	______	______
______________________________	______	______	______
______________________________	______	______	______
______________________________	______	______	______
______________________________	______	______	______

Write about how using helpful, neutral, and unhelpful coping skills affected the situation you were in. What were the consequences of acting in these ways?

____

____

... and more to do

Sometimes we do things without realizing the effects our actions have on other people. Over the next week or so, ask the people you trust about the ways you cope when you're having intense feelings. Find out how they see these behaviors affecting you and those around you. Add these behaviors to the list you made on the previous page and decide whether they are helpful, neutral, or unhelpful.

advantages and disadvantages of behaviors 17

for you to know

We often get stuck in patterns of behavior because they become habits. For example, if you've always coped by spending too much time on the computer, you'll continue to cope in that way until you stop to consider whether you want to change what you do. Looking at the advantages and disadvantages of what you do to cope can help you decide if these are behaviors you want, or need, to change.

This wasn't the first time Trina had impulsively taken an overdose of her medications. Even though she wasn't trying to kill herself, she didn't know how else to express the huge amount of pain she was experiencing or how else to ask for help. When she got into a situation where her emotions were so intense, her automatic reaction tended to be some sort of self-harming behavior, like taking too many pills.

Her counselor asked her to make a list of the advantages and disadvantages of her usual reactions. Seeing it written down that way would make it easier for her to decide whether the behaviors were something she wanted to change.

for you to do

Look back at the behaviors you listed in Activity 16. Choose one that you identified as unhelpful and write it here:

____

Write down any advantages of engaging in this behavior (use another sheet of paper if you don't have enough room).

__________________________ __________________________

__________________________ __________________________

__________________________ __________________________

Next, write down any disadvantages of engaging in this behavior (use another sheet of paper if you need more room).

__________________________ __________________________

__________________________ __________________________

__________________________ __________________________

Now think about this behavior from a different perspective: what are the advantages of *not* engaging in the behavior?

__________________________ __________________________

__________________________ __________________________

__________________________ __________________________

Finally, can you think of disadvantages of *not* engaging in the behavior?

_______________ _______________

_______________ _______________

_______________ _______________

How did you feel about this exercise? Was it easy or hard for you to think of advantages and disadvantages of this behavior?

____

____

____

It is usually helpful if you give yourself at least a few days to do this exercise, to make sure that you're carefully thinking about the advantages and disadvantages of each behavior. Over the next week, come back to your lists and see if you can add more advantages and disadvantages. You can also do more lists, for the other behaviors you identified in Activity 16 as unhelpful.

... and more to do

Your responses to these additional questions can help you break out of any current patterns of unhelpful behavior you may have.

How does engaging in this behavior help you work toward your goals?

How does this behavior prevent you from reaching your goals?

What impact is this behavior having on you and on how you feel about yourself?

What impact is this behavior having on the people you care about?

If your best friend were engaging in this behavior, what would you say to him or her?

learning new ways to cope 18

for you to know

The main goal of healthy coping skills is to help you get through a crisis situation without making things worse. These skills probably won't solve the problem for you, and they won't take away the pain. What they will do is give you a break from the painful thoughts and emotions so that you can get to your wise self for help.

Trina knew that her self-destructive behavior was burning out the people who really cared about her. She could see that they were getting frustrated with her seeming inability to act in constructive ways when she was in a crisis. Her sister didn't talk to her as often as she used to, and when Trina was feeling sad or angry, her friends would stop returning her calls and would avoid spending time with her at school.

She knew she had to get herself out of the pattern she had been stuck in for so long and she began trying to use healthier coping skills. She started to keep a journal where she would write about her feelings rather than venting them to anyone who would listen. She also used her mindfulness skills more often so that she could recognize when her mood was starting to shift and ask for help sooner rather than waiting until she was in the middle of a crisis and trying to hurt herself.

When Trina first started trying to change her behavior, she wasn't able to do it all the time, but as she kept at it, she found that at least sometimes she could act in healthier ways. This showed the people who really cared about her that she was working hard; it gave them hope, and they were able to become more supportive of her efforts.

for you to do

Following is a list of skills that will help you to distract your mind from the problem you're having, and the pain it's causing. Check off or highlight the ones that you do already and then make note of the ones that you could do to distract yourself during a crisis. There are spaces at the end for you to add your own ideas.

Talk to a friend.

Go for a walk.

Ride your bike.

Go skateboarding.

Take a hot bath.

Play with your pet.

Watch television.

Play video games.

Check Facebook.

Check your e-mail.

Do homework.

Listen to music.

Go for a jog.

Go swimming.

Visit a friend.

Go skiing or snowboarding.

Watch a movie.

Scrapbook.

Look at photographs.

Do a crossword puzzle.

Eat your favorite food.

Bake cookies.

Find a fun ring tone for your cell.

Fly a kite.

Journal.

Write a poem.

Go rollerblading.

Go to the beach.

Knit.

Listen to a relaxation CD.

Surf the Internet.

Play a musical instrument.

Play a sport you enjoy.

Play Wii.

Go to the mall.

Go somewhere you'll be around other people, like a park or zoo.

Organize part or all of your room.

Dance.

Go to a museum.

Invite a friend over.

Download some iTunes.

Do something nice for your family or a friend.

Light some candles.

____

____

____

____

____

. . . and more to do

Have you ever noticed how hard it is to think straight when you're in a crisis? The emotions can be so intense that it feels like your head is spinning and you can't think of what to do to help yourself.

Take out a blank piece of paper and start making your own list of ways to distract yourself. Then, when your emotions become really intense, pull out your list, and do the first activity. If that doesn't distract you for very long, move on to the next one. Make your list as long as possible so that you don't run out of ways to distract yourself. Keep adding to your list whenever you think of a new activity that will distract you.

19 creating a crisis plan

for you to know

A crisis plan helps you identify some of your triggers, signs that you need help, and things you can do to help yourself when you're feeling really intense emotions. Having a plan in place makes it easier for you to help yourself when you're in a crisis. It also lets other people know what to do to help you.

It's not always easy to get out of a crisis on your own, especially when you have other challenges, like bipolar disorder, that make it more difficult for you to manage your emotions.

Trina completed a crisis plan, and by being able to identify her triggers and use the skills she included in her plan, she was able to show the people she loved that she was working very hard on acting in healthier ways.

She kept her plan visible by pinning it to the bulletin board on her bedroom wall. Seeing it there, Trina was able to stop herself from acting impulsively; instead, she would use some of the distracting skills she had outlined for herself. The crisis plan also showed her support people what they could do to help Trina be more effective in her life.

for you to do

Over the next week or so, complete your crisis plan using the following form. Then think about people in your life whom you trust, and who you think could help you in a crisis. If it's comfortable for you, give them copies of your plan so that if you do need to call them for help, they'll have some ideas about how they can best help you.

Crisis Plan

Name: ______________________________ Date: ________________

These are my risk factors or triggers (for example, not getting enough sleep, having too much work to do, too much noise and chaos):

- ______________________________
- ______________________________
- ______________________________
- ______________________________
- ______________________________

When I am becoming ill or getting into a crisis, these are some of the signs or symptoms I experience (for example, racing thoughts and difficulties concentrating, isolating myself, staying in my room all day):

- ______________________________
- ______________________________
- ______________________________
- ______________________________
- ______________________________

These are my current crisis patterns:

Physical (for example, I start sleeping more or less; I can't concentrate as well)

____

____

____

Emotional (for example, I become more irritable, sad, tearful)

____

____

____

Behavioral (for example, I start using drugs or alcohol; I withdraw from others)

____

____

____

I can do these things to help distract myself from the crisis (review your list from Activity 18):

__________________ __________________ __________________

__________________ __________________ __________________

__________________ __________________ __________________

__________________ __________________ __________________

__________________ __________________ __________________

These are my key support people:

Name	Phone Number	When to Call
______________	______________	______________
______________	______________	______________
______________	______________	______________
______________	______________	______________
______________	______________	______________

This is the local crisis line to call when no one else is available (like in the middle of the night):

____

This additional information might be useful for people to know so that they can help me (for example, my goals, people and things that are important to me, my hobbies and interests):

____

____

____

Conditions that may require hospital support (for example, if my behavior becomes dangerous, if I become suicidal):

____

____

____

Names and phone numbers of important people:

Psychiatrist: ______________________________

Family doctor: ______________________________

Case manager or other involved professionals: ______________________________

____

Parents or other caregivers: ______________________________

____

Anything else that might be helpful:

____

____

____

____

____

... and more to do

Your plan is a great place to write down all the things you can do to help yourself in a crisis so you don't engage in those old behaviors that end up making things worse. Quite often a crisis is difficult to get through but won't require you to be hospitalized. But for those (hopefully rare) times when things get out of control and you need professional help, this crisis plan will also be useful.

Remember that asking for help is a sign of strength, not weakness. If you experience thoughts of suicide, reach out to a trusted adult in your life immediately. You don't have to deal with this alone!

20 substance use and problem behaviors

for you to know

You may find that drinking, using drugs, or engaging in other potentially addictive behaviors like gambling, gaming, and sex helps you cope with daily stress and provides an escape from your problems. Having a diagnosis of bipolar disorder can make your life even more complicated, which means there is an even higher chance of you turning to these kinds of behaviors in your efforts to feel better. But after some time, you'll find that these things don't really help you. Instead, your problems are likely to get even bigger because you aren't dealing with them. Also, the behaviors themselves become problems that can get in the way of what is important to you.

Jon played baseball and was an excellent science student. He had even received a baseball scholarship to the college that was his first choice. Just before graduation, he had his first manic episode and was diagnosed with bipolar disorder. He felt like his life had been turned upside down. His mom was terrified and couldn't talk about it with him without crying. He didn't think he could talk about it with his friends or with anyone else.

During breaks from studying, Jon had played online poker, but he had never bet money before, and gambling had never gotten in the way of the things he valued and wanted for himself. But after he was diagnosed with bipolar disorder, he found himself on the Internet more and more, and he started to bet money. He ended up regularly borrowing money from his friends so he could keep playing. After a while, he owed his friends so much money that he began to avoid them because he couldn't pay them back.

The gambling continued to become more and more powerful in his life. Soon it took up so much time that Jon was put on suspension from his baseball team for not showing up to practice. His grades were suffering and he was in danger of losing his scholarship. Jon had never meant for this to happen, but his gambling had become an addiction.

for you to do

Look at these illustrations and answer the questions for each.

What purpose does the drug seem to serve for the girl in the situation on the left?

____

____

What purpose does the drug seem to serve for the girl in the situation on the right?

____

____

. . . and more to do

Consider any behaviors you rely on that may be causing you problems, such as using drugs, gambling, or surfing the Internet, and write them in the space provided. While it's most helpful if you can write these down, if you're uncomfortable doing that, you can think of the list in your head.

- ______________________________
- ______________________________
- ______________________________
- ______________________________

How are these behaviors helpful to you?

____

____

What problems do these behaviors cause for you?

____

____

If you were unable to come up with any behaviors you think are problematic, ask someone you trust if they can think of any and for what purpose they see you using these behaviors.

reasons for substance use and problem behaviors 21

for you to know

Substances and behaviors that people come to rely on or become addicted to often serve a purpose. At the same time though, these behaviors usually have a negative impact on their lives.

If you have turned to a potentially problematic behavior, you may find that it helps in the short run. For example, it may be a way for you to avoid uncomfortable emotions for a while, or it may make you feel physically or emotionally well. The story of Jon, in Activity 20, is an example. At first, gambling was just something fun for Jon to do. But after a while, he began to use gambling as a way of avoiding the pain in his life. When he was gambling, he had fun and felt excited, which distracted him from the anger, fear, and disappointment he felt about having bipolar disorder.

Just as it's important to know the long-term consequences of any problem behaviors you engage in, it's also important for you to be aware of the reasons why you're turning to these problematic behaviors.

for you to do

Here are some behaviors and substances people can come to rely on. See if you can match each one with some short-term benefits and long-term consequences that can result; write the letters of the corresponding benefits and consequences in the spaces provided. Some of the benefits and consequences may apply to more than one behavior or substance.

Behaviors and Substances

Alcohol ______________________________

Internet surfing ______________________

Gambling ____________________________

Ecstasy ______________________________

Marijuana ____________________________

Playing video games __________________

Sexual activity (online or in person) ____________________________

Possible Benefits

a. feeling more relaxed

b. feeling more confident

c. forgetting about problems

d. fitting in with friends

e. winning money

f. feeling energized

g. feeling happy

h. sleeping better

i. concentrating better

j. escaping problems for a while

k. slowing racing thoughts

l. helping you be more social

Possible Negative Consequences

1. skipping class or failing
2. triggering a manic episode
3. getting shaky when not using
4. thinking about it all the time
5. losing friends
6. owing money
7. having arguments
8. feeling out of control
9. developing health problems (infections, etc.)
10. feeling guilty
11. interfering with medication
12. experiencing psychotic symptoms (hallucinations, delusions)

List any other short-term benefits you can think of here:

____

____

____

____

List other long-term consequences you can think of here:

____

____

____

____

... and more to do

It can be really hard to look at difficult parts of your life or at the things you are doing that you don't feel good about. Or maybe you don't think a particular behavior is a problem at all, even though it is causing problems in your life (for example, in your relationship with your parents).

But when behaviors become problems, it's really important to take an honest look at them and the negative impact they are having. Just because you do things that you don't necessarily like, or that others may judge you for, doesn't mean there is something "wrong" with you. But you do need to work at stopping these behaviors, so try to be open-minded and honest with yourself.

Here's an exercise to help you. Imagine that you are your best friend or someone else who really cares about you, like your brother or sister, parent, or even your pet. Write a letter to yourself from that person's (or animal's) perspective, talking about the behaviors or substances you are using to cope and how they affect you and your relationships. Use another piece of paper if you need more space.

thinking about things differently 22

for you to know

People often have mixed thoughts and feelings about their substance use or problem behaviors. Don't forget that while the behavior is problematic, it's also been serving a purpose. It can be very difficult to change a behavior that appears to have helped you in some ways. It's also likely that the behavior has a sense of comfort attached to it, since you've probably relied on it for some time, and it's familiar to you. Not having all the information, or having inaccurate information about something, can also get in the way of your being able to make decisions from your wise self. By thinking about these problem behaviors in different ways, you can assess if they are actually helping you or causing more problems for you in the long run.

Jon's mom thought he might be gambling online and started to make comments about how much time he was on the computer. Jon thought she was overreacting and felt irritated by her comments, which seemed like nagging to him. They had arguments about it, and he'd yell at her to stop bothering him about it because it wasn't a big deal. He'd also lie to her, saying that he wasn't gambling when he really was.

Jon loved the feelings that gambling created and, although he rarely won, the rush when he did was enough to keep him playing. But as he started to lose more and more things that were important to him—friends, self-respect, and the money he had saved to buy a new keyboard—and to feel the shame and fear that came along with these losses, things started to change. It was like there were two different realities, as if he were seeing gambling through two different lenses. All he saw through one lens was how wonderful, exciting, and harmless gambling was. But when he looked through another lens, he was able to see the problems with it, too.

As he experienced gambling in this more accurate way, he began to be open to the possibility that his own gambling was actually a problem. With this new perspective, Jon was able to challenge his experiences of gambling. He could remind himself of the problems it caused and was able to start to limit how much he gambled and to do other more helpful things to feel better.

for you to do

What are some ideas you have about the substances you are using or your problem behaviors? Some common ones are included below; use the blank lines to add your own.

- It can't hurt me if I only do it a little.
- It's what I need to do to be accepted by my friends.
- I'm not hurting anyone.
- Everyone does it.
- ____
- ____
- ____
- ____
- ____
- ____

Really think about each of your ideas. Read; research on the Internet; or talk to your doctor, psychotherapist, family, friends, or anyone else you trust, in order to get a variety of opinions about the issue. Then, using your wise self, put an "X" next to the beliefs you hold about the idea that are not really accurate.

Now, see if you can counter each of the inaccurate beliefs. For example, if you believe that "everyone does it," your research may have shown you that "not everyone drinks just because they want to feel accepted." Write these new, more accurate statements here, using more paper if you need to:

- ____
- ____
- ____
- ____
- ____
- ____
- ____
- ____
- ____
- ____
- ____

... and more to do

Return to Activity 3 for a moment and review the goals and preferences you identified for yourself. How might your substance use or problem behaviors get in the way of your ability to meet these goals?

____

____

____

In addition to the suggestions below, what other steps could you take to stop substances and behaviors from becoming a problem and preventing you from reaching your goals? If this is difficult to figure out, think about what you would suggest to a friend like Jon.

- Speak to your parents, guidance counselor, religious leader, or someone else you trust.
- Find and call a social service agency for help.
- Find an online chat room where you can anonymously ask others where they've gone for help with similar problems. As with anything on the Internet, of course, you need to be cautious; make sure any sites you participate in are run by reliable organizations.
- ____
- ____
- ____
- ____

how you learn about yourself 23

for you to know

The way you think and feel about yourself is influenced by many things, including messages you get from the media, your family, and your friends. These messages often come from ideas that are based on your skin color, gender, culture, religion, ability, or sexual orientation. They can be obvious or subtle, and they usually give you ideas about things like how likeable, acceptable, or smart you are. After a while, you can begin to believe these messages, even if they aren't helpful.

Growing up, Akisha had lived in a small town and was the only African American kid in her school. Some of the children called her racist names. When she read stories for school, the pictures in them were only of white girls and boys. Akisha grew up feeling different from the other kids, out of place, and unacceptable because of the obvious and subtle messages she received about herself.

In ninth grade, Akisha and her family moved to a large city, and for the first time she saw other teens who looked like her. She made friends with all kinds of kids and felt like she finally belonged. She began to embrace her African heritage more fully. A new story of her began to emerge. She discovered that she cared deeply about accepting people and treating them fairly. She joined a school group committed to promoting acceptance of diversity and became a leader in her school.

Then Akisha was diagnosed with bipolar disorder and once again she found herself feeling like an outsider. She began to avoid others because her belief that she was unacceptable and her feelings of shame had resurfaced. It was even worse for her than when she was in grade school because messages about this disorder were being attached to her, like that people with bipolar disorder are "crazy" or "sick" or "scary." Akisha's favorite teacher noticed what was happening and spoke to her parents, who brought Akisha to a group for kids dealing with bipolar disorder. This group helped her reclaim her view of herself as a committed and caring person with wonderful leadership qualities!

for you to do

Use your imagination. What were some of the messages Akisha got about herself as a child?

____

____

____

How did these messages change once Akisha started high school? What were the messages?

____

____

____

Which of the messages above are the "truth" about Akisha?

______ The messages Akisha got when she was in grade school are the truth.

______ The messages Akisha got when she was in high school are the truth.

______ None of the messages about Akisha are *really* "true"; it's what Akisha believes that matters.

Which of these sets of messages would help Akisha feel good about herself, and which "truth" should she pay attention to? Why?

____

____

... and more to do

Think of examples of messages people in your life get about themselves. For each message, tell what its origin is and how you think it impacts that person. One has been done for you as an example.

Person: My friend Leah Message: Household chores are her job.

Origin: Her brother, her father, and society say that household chores are women's work, not men's.

Impact: Leah has to do all the household chores. She doesn't have much time to do the things she likes and she feels resentful a lot of the time.

Person: ______________ Message: ______________

____

Origin: ______________ Impact: ______________

____

Person: ______________ Message: ______________

____

Origin: ______________ Impact: ______________

____

Person: ______________ Message: ______________

____

Origin: ______________ Impact: ______________

____

24 messages about who you are

for you to know

The messages you get from others can influence the way you think and feel about yourself, which, in turn, can influence your mood. Looking at the messages you receive from others and how they influence what you think and feel about yourself is an important step toward improving your self-esteem.

Jonas didn't have many friends at school, and people called him names like "geek" or "nerd" because his grades were in the high 90s. He was also made fun of for having bipolar disorder. For the past few years, he'd had problems with bullies who would steal from him and push him around. He dreaded going to school, which created a lot of anxiety for him and often triggered depressive episodes.

When Jonas began to miss a lot of school, his father brought him to see a psychotherapist. Through their conversations, Jonas was able to see how the bullying affected him. It communicated messages that there was something wrong with him and that he was helpless to do anything about how the bullies were treating him. What was more harmful, Jonas realized, was that he himself had come to believe these messages! He didn't even need the bullies to be around for him to feel bullied.

Given Jonas's experiences, it made a lot of sense that he would feel depressed and anxious about going to school. These messages began to take up so much space in Jonas's experiences of himself and school that he forgot positive things: his satisfaction and pride when he got a good grade, his friends in math class who also cared about school and got high grades, and how much he liked his science teacher, who seemed to really appreciate his abilities.

When he recognized the power bullying was having over him, Jonas felt ready to take back his life. He did this in small steps, using skills he practiced with his psychotherapist. When he noticed anxiety symptoms, like dizziness, he would slow down his breathing and reassure himself. In the mornings when depression told him it was going to be a horrible day, he talked back to it, saying, "You don't know that, and even if it is I can handle it. I always do." He also decided to join the karate club, thinking this would help him feel more secure physically.

Jonas still felt anxious and had low moods, but they no longer interfered with what he wanted for himself.

for you to do

Think about the different messages that exist about you and write them in the spaces provided. Some of these may have to do with the way you look, your personality, or the way you behave. Some possibilities are listed below.

nice	weird	selfish
moody	caring	smart
__________	__________	__________
__________	__________	__________
__________	__________	__________

These messages may have come from television, movies, or magazines. Maybe they came from people in your life. These words may have been actually said to you, or they may have been communicated by how people acted toward you. It's possible that you've come to believe some of these messages and to think them yourself.

Look at the messages you've written above, and choose the five that most influence how you think or feel about yourself. For each of these, write down its origin (where it came from) and its impact (how it makes you think and feel about yourself, and how you act):

1. Message: ______________________________

   Origin: ______________________________

   Impact: ______________________________

2. Message: ______________________________

   Origin: ______________________________

   Impact: ______________________________

3. Message: ______________________________

   Origin: ______________________________

   Impact: ______________________________

4. Message: ______________________________

   Origin: ______________________________

   Impact: ______________________________

5. Message: ______________________________

   Origin: ______________________________

   Impact: ______________________________

... and more to do

Messages often begin early in life. Looking at the messages you've written above, when do you think you first began experiencing them?

___

___

How do you feel when you think about or believe these messages?

___

___

Which messages about yourself would you like to keep?

- ___
- ___
- ___
- ___
- ___

Which messages about yourself would you like to let go of?

- ___
- ___
- ___
- ___
- ___

In North America, for example, the dominant culture is white, heterosexual, Christian, male, with no physical disabilities. If you are different in some way from this, you've likely experienced some negative messages about who you are.

Think of the messages you have received about your bipolar diagnosis, sexual identity, culture, skin color, religion, or physical status. Choose one of those aspects and tell what messages exist about it.

____

____

____

How do these messages affect how you think and feel about yourself?

____

____

____

25 how words impact your self-esteem

for you to know

Some of the messages you receive may have a negative influence over how you think and feel about yourself. The good news is that you can make changes to limit the effects of these messages and improve the relationship you have with yourself. A big part of mental wellness is having good self-esteem, which comes, in part, from the way you think about and talk to yourself.

Unfortunately, many of us have grown up hearing negative judgments and messages on a regular basis. You can probably recall people (parents, teachers, friends) saying things to you like, "That was good," "You're being bad," or "I can't believe you did that. What were you thinking?" If you've heard many of these messages in your life, you may have taken on this way of evaluating yourself. People are almost always having internal conversations with themselves, which is referred to as self-talk. Your self-talk—what you tell yourself—may be a clue to whether or not you are your own harshest critic.

for you to do

Some people call themselves "stupid" or talk down to themselves in other ways. These self-judgments can perpetuate the negative messages they receive and strengthen their belief in them. What things do you say to yourself that keep negative messages going?

____

____

When you judge yourself this way, what feelings come up for you? List your judgments and feelings below.

Self-Judgment	**Feeling**
"I'm stupid; I can't do this."	Anger, sadness
"Having bipolar disorder means I'm crazy."	Anxiety, anger
____________________	____________________
____________________	____________________
____________________	____________________
____________________	____________________
____________________	____________________
____________________	____________________
____________________	____________________
____________________	____________________

Now that you're aware of the feelings that come up when you judge yourself this way, see if you can come up with more neutral or gentler ways of speaking to yourself. This is called being nonjudgmental. To be nonjudgmental, you need to stick to describing the situation and how you feel about it, staying away from judging yourself. Look at the first two examples and then complete the rest on your own.

You have trouble with your math homework.

Self-judgment: I'm stupid; I can't do this.

Nonjudgmental statement: I'm feeling frustrated because I'm finding this difficult and I'm taking it out on myself.

When you have a depressive episode, you often miss chorus practice.

Self-judgment: I'm crazy.

Nonjudgmental statement: Having bipolar disorder means it is sometimes harder for me to keep up with activities.

You get a D on an essay you wrote.

Self-judgment: ____________________

Nonjudgmental statement: ____________________

____

You stop taking your medication and end up being hospitalized for a manic or depressive episode.

Self-judgment: ____________________

Nonjudgmental statement: ____________________

____

You have an argument with your best friend because you backed out on plans you had made.

Self-judgment: ____________________

Nonjudgmental statement: ____________________

____

... and more to do

Self-judgments can be difficult to catch, especially if they've been going on for a long time and have become a habit. Start paying more attention to times when you are your own harshest critic and to the kinds of judgments you make. Remember, judgments do not represent the truth. Instead, they are simply a way you are thinking about yourself or the situation. Changing these to neutral, nonjudgmental, or supportive thoughts can reduce the painful feelings you have in your life and help you feel more content and confident.

26 developing a new story of you

for you to know

The kinds of things you like to do and the things that are important to you are clues to your unique qualities, commitments, and strengths. It's important to get to know and understand these so you can develop a strong and supportive relationship with yourself.

Lin had always enjoyed playing hockey. She could remember being in grade school, playing hockey with the boys in her class at recess. She also remembered the times her teacher had told her she should be spending more time with the girls in her class instead of playing hockey with the boys so much.

Over the years, Lin received similar messages from her family, friends, and the media: hockey is for boys, so she shouldn't play it and she shouldn't want to play it. But because she continued to love the game and still wanted to play, Lin sometimes thought there must be something wrong with her and she would feel ashamed.

She also knew what she liked about hockey: the teamwork and having to work hard. Her enjoyment told her that working with others was something she valued. Her willingness to work hard was a sign of her determination and motivation. She preferred these messages, and they were much truer for her. She felt better about herself when she was in touch with these messages.

for you to do

Lin's situation is just one example of how your likes and dislikes, and the messages you receive about them, can affect the way you think and feel about yourself. In the spaces provided, write down some of your likes (for example, rollercoasters, music, and chatting on Facebook) and dislikes (for example, scary movies and shopping).

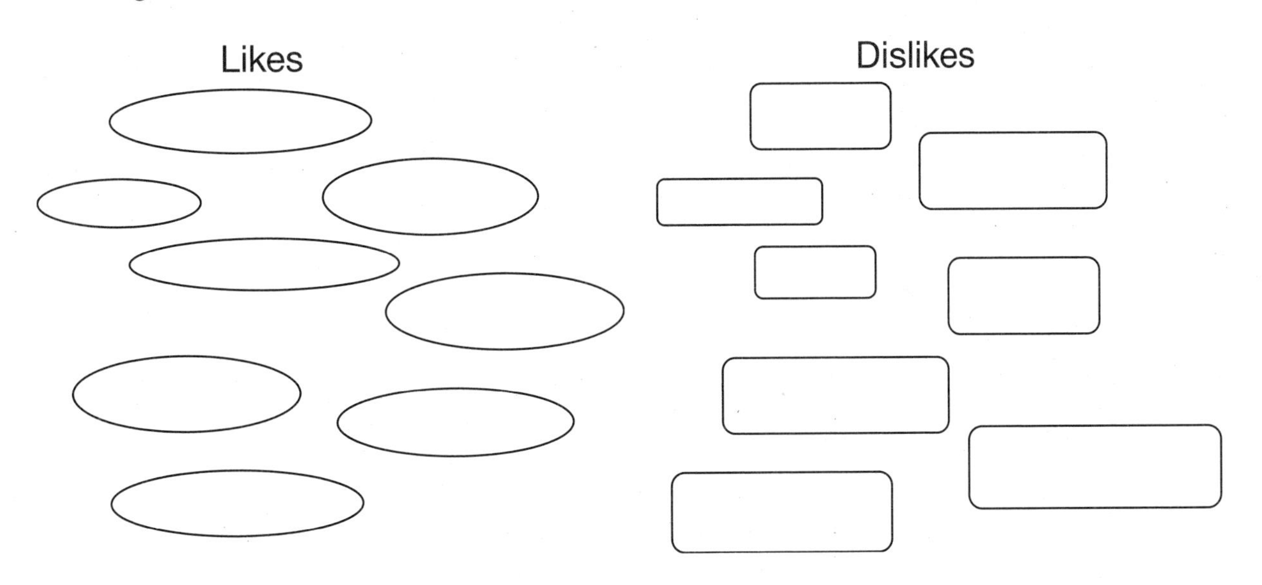

What do your likes and dislikes tell you about you? For example, liking rollercoasters might mean you are courageous, while disliking shopping could mean you prefer to save your money.

____

____

____

If you are having a hard time answering this, ask some people you trust to share their impressions. Write down what they say about your strengths and what they think is important to you.

___

___

___

Now think about some of the different aspects of yourself. Describe yourself (your qualities, what's important to you, things you'd like to change) in relation to each area, and include your feelings about it. If you notice negative judgments coming up, put parentheses around them to keep them separate. Then try to rewrite them more descriptively and without judgment.

Me as a friend: ___

___

___

___

Me with bipolar disorder: ___

___

___

___

Me using substances (or other problem behaviors): ___

___

___

___

My sexual self: ______________________________

____

____

____

Me as a student or employee: ______________________________

____

____

____

Other thoughts about myself: ______________________________

____

____

____

... and more to do

Now you have an idea of how you think and feel about some aspects of yourself that come up in different situations or contexts. Over the coming days, pay attention to how you think about and talk to yourself, especially in relation to those things that you don't like, and practice being less judgmental and more kind and gentle with yourself.

accepting painful situations 27

for you to know

The word "acceptance" does not mean that you ***approve*** of something, that you like it, or that you don't want it to change. It simply means that you recognize or acknowledge that this is your reality. In other words, you tell yourself: "It is what it is."

It's often hard to accept that certain painful things have happened or are happening in our lives. Instead of accepting, we tend to fight these things, usually by trying to deny them in some way. "It's not fair," "This shouldn't have happened," 'Why me?"—these are all examples of what we might say to ourselves when we're not accepting. When we don't accept these situations, however, we end up triggering more painful emotions for ourselves.

for you to do

In the space below, write down some painful situations you've experienced and were able to accept. We've started you off with some examples, but if you can't recall a situation like this, ask someone you trust for help.

- The fact that you have bipolar disorder
- The death of a friend, family member, pet, or someone else you care about
- The end of a relationship with someone you really cared about
- ____
- ____
- ____
- ____

Next, choose one of these situations and think back to how it felt when this event had just happened. The pain was probably pretty intense, and you may recall that you didn't accept the situation at first. You might also recall having done some things that you later regretted, such as using drugs or alcohol or turning to other problematic behaviors. Write about your experience with fighting the reality of that situation, in as much detail as you can recall (use more paper if you need to):

____

____

____

____

____

Write about your experience of accepting this same situation. Include whatever you can recall, in as much detail as possible (use extra paper if you run out of room). For example, what started you down the path of acceptance? Was it something someone said to you, a thought you had yourself, an event? What was different for you once you were able to accept? Did your emotions change? Did how you think about the situation change?

____

____

____

____

____

____

… and more to do

Hopefully you've just seen that while acceptance doesn't make the pain of a difficult situation go away, it does reduce the amount of extra pain you have about that situation. Make a list of situations that you still need to work on accepting. Once you've listed all the situations you can think of, rank them in order from the least painful (1) to the most painful. You'll learn about what to do with these situations in the next activity.

Situation	**Rank**
______________________________	____
______________________________	____
______________________________	____
______________________________	____
______________________________	____
______________________________	____
______________________________	____

practicing acceptance 28

for you to know

Accepting reality will reduce how often you experience painful emotions, but it's a very difficult thing to do. The more painful a situation, the harder it is to accept and the longer it will likely take you. It's important to keep in mind that accepting reality isn't about getting rid of your emotions; although your pain might decrease when you start accepting something, it's not likely to go away, since the situation itself is painful.

To practice acceptance, you need to decide that you want to work on accepting a situation. If you decide it's worth the effort, you need to make a commitment to yourself that you're going to start trying to accept that situation. Next, you notice whenever you're not accepting it—when you hear yourself fighting that reality. And finally, without judging yourself for continuing to not accept the experience, you reach for acceptance.

The process is kind of like having an argument with yourself: you hear your mind fighting the reality, you purposefully tell yourself that you're working on accepting that reality, and you reach for acceptance in whatever way works best for you—whether it's simply saying to yourself, "It is what it is," or perhaps picturing yourself in your mind's eye, turning down the pathway to acceptance.

for you to do

Look back at Activity 27, where you listed and ranked painful situations you believe you need to accept. Practicing with a situation that's a bit less painful makes it easier to see that you can get to acceptance, so you'll start with the situation you ranked as #1.

Write it here: ______________________________

How do you know when you're not accepting this reality? Do you say certain things to yourself (like "It's not fair" or "It shouldn't have happened")? Do you engage in certain behaviors (like throwing a temper tantrum or hiding in your room)?

____

____

What can you say to yourself to help you accept this situation?

- It is what it is.
- I accept the reality that I have bipolar disorder.
- ______________________________
- ______________________________
- ______________________________

The coping skills discussed earlier in Activity 18 will also help you get through these difficult times in the short run. Acceptance is really a longer-term skill, but if you practice this skill regularly, you will eventually have fewer crises to deal with.

... and more to do

At first you may only be able to accept this situation for a few minutes at a time, but once you've been working on acceptance for a while, you'll find that you're able to do it for longer periods. You might also find that you get to acceptance with the situation, but then something happens to make you not accept it again. That's okay—just go back over the steps outlined earlier and keep reaching for acceptance.

When you feel you've made headway with this situation, and when you're comfortable, move on to the situation you ranked as #2. Answer the same questions you did for the first situation, and then begin the process of accepting this reality.

29 accepting your emotions

for you to know

You've just learned the importance of accepting realities that are painful in your life. Equally important is learning to accept painful emotions without judging them in order to reduce the amount of time you're spending acting only from your emotional self.

Just as they refuse to accept painful situations, many people fight painful emotions, and the result is the same: more pain. The more emotions you have, the harder it is to think straight and problem-solve in order to help yourself. Think of these emotions as being like quicksand: The more you struggle against the quicksand and try to get out, the deeper it sucks you in. When you stop struggling, the quicksand doesn't spit you back out, but it does stop sucking you under. Likewise, when you stop fighting the painful emotions in your life, they won't just miraculously disappear, but you will gain some breathing space to think about what to do next. JT's story is an example.

JT often felt anxious when he was with his friends. He had been seeing a therapist to help him with his anxiety problems and was planning on trying out some newly learned skills at a party he was going to. As the party drew closer, though, JT felt really nervous about going; he was worried he would say or do something that would make him look stupid. Noticing this anxiety, JT began to judge himself for it, thinking, "This is stupid! Here I've been doing all this work, trying to do things to help myself, but I'm still anxious. I'm such a loser!"

These kinds of thoughts about his anxiety, and about himself for feeling anxious, only triggered more emotions in JT. Now, not only was he still anxious about the party, but he was also angry at himself for feeling anxious.

for you to do

Think about the last time you felt anxious or fearful. What were your thoughts about feeling this way? For example, did you think you were "wrong" because you were anxious or that you "shouldn't" feel that way? Did you struggle against the feeling or were you able to accept it? (If you're unable to recall thoughts about your emotions, come back to this exercise after you experience each emotion again, so that it's fresh in your mind.)

____

____

Now answer the same questions for the feeling of anger: ____________________

____

And sadness: ____

____

And jealousy: ____

____

Although it's most often the painful emotions we struggle against, sometimes there are other emotions that we fight as well. For example, many people with bipolar disorder start to feel anxious if they feel happy or excited, because this could be a sign of a coming manic episode. Write down any other emotions you struggle with:

____

____

____

Now think about these emotions. What happens when you fight them? For example, do you feel less pain or more? Does the emotion hang around or fade away? Do you notice that additional emotions come up?

____

____

What can you say to yourself to help you be more accepting of these emotions?

- It is what it is.
- It's okay for me to feel this way.
- ____
- ____
- ____

... and more to do

For the next few weeks, be more mindful of how you respond to your emotions. Notice whether you are struggling against them or accepting them. For those that you're fighting, see if you can start to change the way you think about them by not judging them and just accepting them as natural human emotions.

30 relationships with others

for you to know

Relationships and feeling connected to others are an important and basic part of life. Some relationships are close connections and others distant; some may be satisfying and others not. Even when you are not actually with people, you think about them or are influenced by them and, in this way, you are still connected. Your relationships influence your experiences of yourself, others, and the world.

Jacob liked to think of himself as a guy who didn't need anyone. When he was young, he had been very close to his younger brother and had a group of boys that he spent a lot of time with. His dad had left when Jacob was ten, and that's when things started to change. His mother was very sad and angry, and they had a lot of money problems. Jacob felt sad, and he missed his dad very much. He also felt scared and lonely. But he thought that he should keep his feelings and his questions about what happened to himself. He didn't want to upset his mom even more by telling her how much pain he was in.

Over time, Jacob learned to rely on himself. He got himself and his brother ready for school, did his homework, and sometimes had to make dinner if his mom worked late. When he was diagnosed with bipolar disorder, he found it very difficult to deal with on his own. His mom knew he was struggling and she worried about him, but their relationship had changed. He wasn't used to opening up to her, and he didn't think he wanted her help.

While the belief that he had only himself to rely on came as a result of his earlier experiences, his independent approach to life became an obstacle to his getting and staying well, which he wanted very much to do. Things had changed, and now Jacob needed help from others to ensure he would have the life he wanted.

for you to do

Put a check next to the beliefs that fit best with your ideas about relationships.

Here are some common beliefs about relationships:

______ Relying on others is a sign of weakness.

______ People need positive connections with others.

______ People can't be trusted.

______ If people don't do what is asked of them, it means they don't care.

______ Relationships are more trouble than they are worth.

______ I am doing as well as I am partly because of the caring people in my life.

______ It's a sign of maturity to ask for help.

Add any others you can think of:

____

____

____

____

Below is a list of ways you may feel and behave when each of your beliefs is most prominent in your mind. Place the corresponding letter(s) next to each belief you've checked above.

a. lonely
b. sad
c. frustrated
d. safe
e. secure
f. happy
g. hopeful
h. isolate myself
i. keep things to myself
j. share my thoughts and feeling
k. talk to friends, family, therapists
l. show I am interested in others
m. talk badly about others
n. ____________________
o. ____________________
p. ____________________

Keeping your goals for yourself in mind, think about how helpful each of your beliefs (and the corresponding feelings and behaviors you identified) is to you. Organize them this way:

Beliefs I prefer to have because they are more helpful to me:

____

____

____

____

____

Beliefs I want to let go of because they are not very helpful to me:

____

____

____

____

____

Your life is influenced by the beliefs you have about relationships. What can you do to keep more connected to the beliefs you prefer to have? We've started you off with some ideas and provided some space for you to add your own strategies. Place a check next to the ones you would like to try.

______ Remind yourself of these beliefs.

______ Try out some opposite behaviors to see what happens. For example, if you would typically keep something in, try saying it out loud.

______ Take a risk with people who are important to you and open up to them.

______ Remember times in the past when you asked for help and it turned out okay.

______ ____

______ ____

______ ____

... and more to do

Check off any new ideas you have developed about relationships as result of your diagnosis. Use the blank lines to add your own ideas.

- ☐ I will need relationships even more now.
- ☐ Some people won't understand but others will.
- ☐ I will never be close to anyone now.
- ☐ If people find out, they won't like me.
- ☐ ____________________
- ☐ ____________________
- ☐ ____________________
- ☐ ____________________

If any of these ideas are interfering with the ideas you prefer to have about relationships, what can you do?

- ☐ Talk to someone you trust about it.
- ☐ ____________________
- ☐ Spend time with your friends anyway.
- ☐ ____________________
- ☐ ____________________
- ☐ ____________________
- ☐ ____________________
- ☐ ____________________

Look back at the messages you wrote about in Activity 24 regarding your bipolar diagnosis, sexual identity, culture, skin color, religion, or physical status. How do the messages that exist about these areas impact your ideas about relationships and their role in your life?

____

____

____

While completing this exercise, you may have noticed that you would like to have more relationships in your life. If this is the case, what could you do to help bring about this change? Look at the suggested possibilities and add your own ideas.

- ☐ Join a club, team, or group.
- ☐ Ask someone you trust to introduce you to new people.
- ☐ ______________________________
- ☐ ______________________________
- ☐ Start accepting invitations from others.
- ☐ Expand your interests so you have some things you can share with new people.
- ☐ ______________________________
- ☐ ______________________________

31 what do you want from your relationships?

for you to know

Ideally, your closest relationships are with people who help you get in touch with your skills and resources. Those people can also help you make good choices for yourself that fit with your preferences and goals. These types of relationships are more satisfying than ones that result in your feeling bad or insecure about yourself, or that influence you to make unwise choices.

Jacob had two friends, Mark and Cam, with whom he grew up. Although they went to different schools, they still kept in touch. Sometimes all three of them would get together to play video games, but Jacob usually spent time with each of them separately because of everyone's busy schedules.

He began to notice that spending time with Mark was not as much fun as it used to be. Mark liked to tease Jacob about things he said or the way he looked. He also insulted Cam when Cam wasn't there. Jacob noticed that he ended up feeling pretty bad about himself after he spent time with Mark. Mark was not someone he could trust, and he decided he would never tell him about having bipolar disorder.

Cam, on the other hand, was someone Jacob felt very comfortable with. He could be himself without having to watch what he said. Cam did not tease him. Cam was also a really good listener who didn't interrupt Jacob, and he would ask Jacob questions about what he was saying.

for you to do

List the important people in your life. You may not always get along with these people or like them, but they still have a big role in your life. (You might want to refer back to Activity 4 to help you with this.)

______________________________	______________________________
______________________________	______________________________
______________________________	______________________________

Although there may be some difficulties because no relationship is perfect, which of these relationships do you feel satisfied with overall? Which ones aren't satisfying to you? Write them in the appropriate column.

Important relationships that feel satisfying	**Important relationships that don't feel very satisfying**
______________________________	______________________________
______________________________	______________________________
______________________________	______________________________
______________________________	______________________________
______________________________	______________________________

For the relationships you placed under the "satisfied" column, what do you find satisfying? Think about what you like about the relationship, how you feel when you are spending time with or thinking about that person, and what skills and qualities that person helps you get in touch with. Some examples are included.

- ☐ I am able to say what's on my mind.
- ☐ The person really listens to me.
- ☐ I feel cared for and accepted.
- ☐ ______________________________
- ☐ ______________________________
- ☐ I can tell this person really likes me.
- ☐ With this person, I feel like my future has hope.
- ☐ ______________________________
- ☐ ______________________________

Now think about the relationships you placed under the "unsatisfied" column. What would you like to change about each of these? We've started you off with some possible examples.

- ☐ I'd like to argue less.
- ☐ I want to trust this person.
- ☐ I want to say what's on my mind.
- ☐ ______________________________
- ☐ ______________________________
- ☐ I want this person to stop criticizing me.
- ☐ I want this person to give me some space.
- ☐ I want us to spend more time together.
- ☐ ______________________________

... and more to do

On a separate piece of paper, write a letter to one of the important people you listed in the "unsatisfied" column. You don't have to send this letter; this is simply an exercise to help you be honest and say what's true for you. Even in unsatisfying relationships, there can be positive aspects, so tell that person what aspects of your relationship you really like. Then write down the things about the relationship that you don't like, that you feel unsatisfied with, or that you'd like to see change. Finally, write down what *you'd* be willing to do differently to contribute to that change. Think about whether you are going to discuss this with the person and, if you are, refer to Activities 33 and 34 to help you communicate effectively.

32 recognizing what you can change and accepting what you can't

for you to know

There are parts of life that you have more control over than others. Going to school, not smoking, and expressing yourself are examples of things you have control over. How other people think, act, or feel, and if it rains are aspects of life you have very little control over. Putting your energy into what you can control rather than what you can't will help you create the changes you want.

When Jacob was diagnosed with bipolar disorder, he felt like he was losing control. It was difficult for him to accept that it was now part of his life and that he could not make it go away. What he did have control over, however, were things like how he was going to live his life: whether he would take his medication, get enough sleep, or be mindful of how he was feeling. When Jacob started to put his energy into things he could control and change, he felt better.

for you to do

The oval on the left represents parts of your life that you have control over and can change. The oval on the right represents parts of your life that you don't have control over and can't change. Write down aspects of your life that you can change and can't change in the appropriate oval.

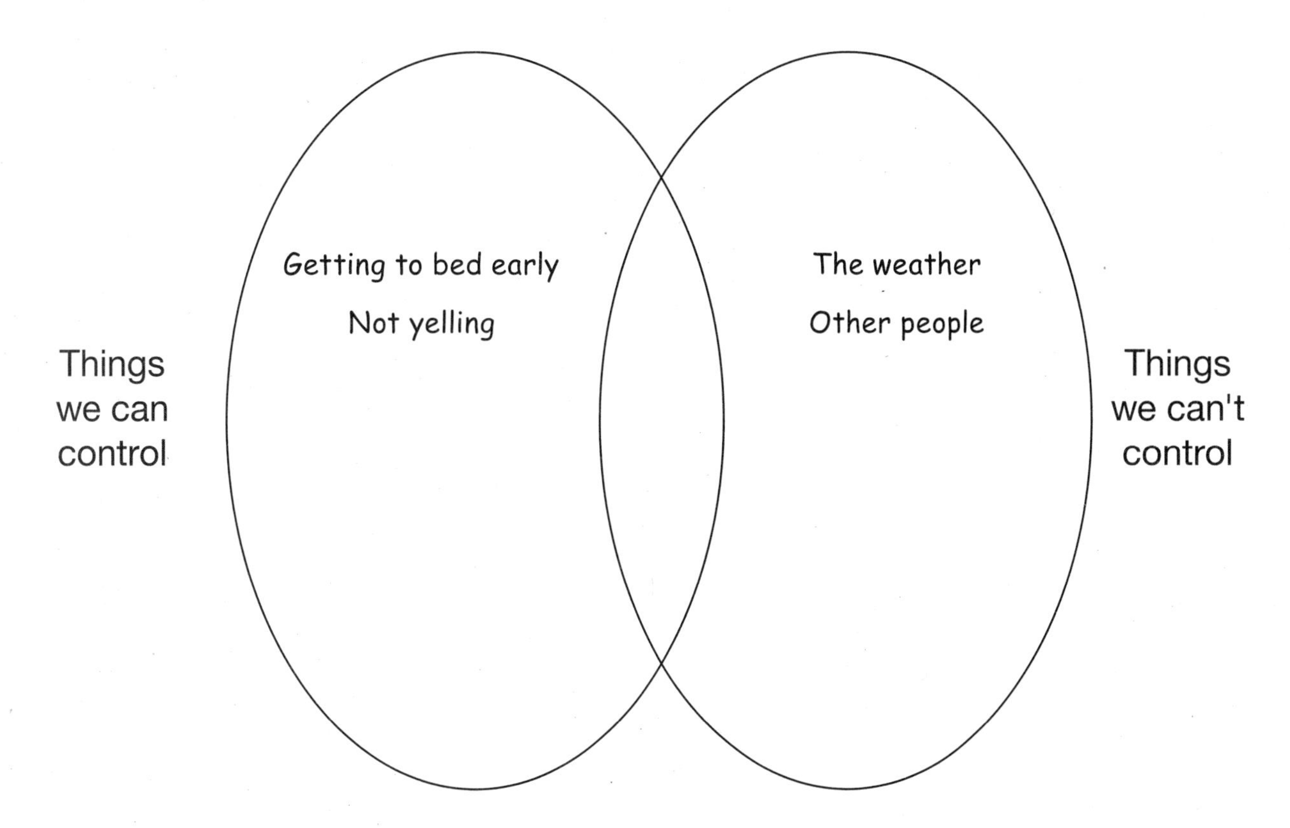

The space where the ovals overlap indicates areas of your life that you can control in part, but not entirely, like relationships. There are aspects of relationships that you have control over and can change and aspects that you have no control over and can't change. This is important to remember, since you might find yourself spending a lot of energy trying to change others because you believe that they are the only ones responsible for any problems in the relationship. That isn't usually the case, except in abusive relationships (for example, where your partner often gets angry with you; tries to control what you do; ignores, swears, or insults you; or hits, pinches, or pushes you around); then the abusive person is the *only one* responsible for the abusive behavior.

Putting your energy into trying to change someone else is not usually helpful. On the other hand, sometimes people think that a relationship will never change. For example, if you think, "My mom will never get it," you might not even try to make things better. What's more helpful is for you to change how you act, think, or feel. When one person makes positive changes, it often leads to positive change in the overall relationship.

List aspects of your relationships you have control over and can change and aspects of relationships you don't have control over and can't change.

Things about my relationships I can change:

- ______________________________
- ______________________________
- ______________________________
- ______________________________

Things about my relationships I can't change:

- ______________________________
- ______________________________
- ______________________________
- ______________________________

... and more to do

Look back at Activity 31 and choose one of the relationships you want to change. What could you do to help bring about the changes you want to see in this relationship?

33 your communication skills

for you to know

Communication is complex and goes beyond just the words you choose. In fact, about 90 percent of what you communicate is nonverbal. It involves the tone and volume of your voice, how quickly you speak, your posture, your use of eye contact, and your facial expression. People are always communicating with each other, and learning how to do it with skill can make your relationships more satisfying.

Tyrell's approach to communicating was, more or less, to keep everything inside. When he was diagnosed with bipolar disorder, he became even more secretive. He believed that he couldn't tell his thoughts and feelings to anyone. He was convinced that no one would understand what he was going through. If someone did something that bothered him, he'd hold in his feelings for as long as he could until he finally exploded in a rage, usually at his mom or brother. This way of communicating did not get Tyrell what he wanted, and it got in the way of his having positive relationships with many people.

for you to do

These communication skills contribute to positive relationships. Put a star beside the ones you already do well and a check beside the ones you'd like to get better at.

____ I speak calmly if I am upset.

____ I firmly ask for what I need or want *and* accept it if the person says no, even if I don't like it.

____ I make requests of people rather than demands.

____ I don't insult or criticize others, even when I am mad at them.

____ I take a break if I'm not able to stay in control and then come back to discuss things when I feel more calm.

____ I avoid saying things like, "You always...," "You never...," or "You should..." when I talk to other people.

____ I say things as simply as possible and don't go on and on.

____ I assume that others want to understand me and I am patient if they don't get it the first time.

____ If the person doesn't get what I am trying to say, I try to explain it differently.

____ I look at the person when I talk.

____ I don't use threatening gestures.

____ I don't try to intimidate others by getting into their physical space.

____ I express my anger to someone I'm angry with rather than spreading rumors or lies about that person on the Internet or at school.

Think about a time when you used one of the skills you checked. How do you think that helped the conversation go as it did?

____

____

____

Now choose one of the skills you would like to get better at. Think of a situation when you could try it. In the space provided, write what you could say in that situation. When you actually do try it, notice how the interaction goes.

____

____

____

Mania or depression may make it hard for you to participate in conversations the way you want to. For example, you might find it difficult to really listen, or you might talk in ways that can hurt your relationship. If that happens, what could you do?

- Tell the person you are not feeling well and ask if you could have the conversation another time.
- Ask someone you trust for help.
- ____
- ____
- ____

. . . and more to do

Assertive statements allow you to express your needs and wants in a respectful way while recognizing that the other person has the right to say yes or no and to agree or disagree with you. Assertive statements generally follow this format:

1. Calmly state your feelings.
2. Identify the person's behavior that is bothering you (an action, not a personal quality).
3. Tell what you'd like to see different.

For example, here is an assertive statement: "I feel irritated when you interrupt me. I would like it if you could listen until I'm finished." The opposite could go something like this: "You're always interrupting me and you don't care about anyone but yourself. I can't stand how selfish you are!" This kind of attacking statement is unlikely to contribute to the change you want. It usually makes people stop listening to what you say and gets them to attack you back or ignore you outright.

Try creating an assertive statement on your own. Briefly write about a situation that has been bothering you that you've experienced with a person in your life:

____

Fill in the following blanks to create an assertive statement you could say to that person.

I feel ____________________ when you ______________________________.

I would like it if you ____.

Even if you make an assertive statement, don't assume that the other person will hear it the way you intended. You might need to restate it calmly. If the person becomes critical of you or dismisses what you've said, walk away from the conversation. You can wait to see if he or she makes the change you've requested. If you don't get the results you're looking for, you can decide whether the relationship is positive and important enough for you to keep, despite the person's behavior.

34 listening to others

for you to know

When a person uses good listening skills, others feel understood and accepted. Even when there are disagreements, being able to really listen and understand is very important in helping to create positive relationships.

Have you ever been talking to someone who was looking around or interrupting you or seemed preoccupied with something else? It's upsetting, isn't it? Often it's frustrating and irritating. Sometimes it can send a message that what you have to say is not important and, even though that's not true, it can feel hurtful. Now imagine what it might be like for another person if it's you who's not paying attention or really listening.

for you to do

Below is a list of listening skills. Put a star next to the ones you already do well and a check next to the ones you'd like to develop.

____ I try to understand what people say to me, even if I disagree.

____ I listen without making faces or rolling my eyes.

____ I let others speak without interrupting.

____ I ask questions if I don't understand.

____ I don't respond by justifying, defending, or rationalizing.

____ I use eye contact to show I am listening.

____ I repeat what I heard the person say and ask if I'm right.

____ I show respect for people even if I don't agree with what they are saying.

____ I show that I empathize with the person speaking by saying something like "That sounds hard" or "I can understand why you feel that way."

____ I ask people if it would be okay to talk about something later if I can't give them my full attention at the time. When I am ready, I follow up.

Think about a time when you used one of the skills you starred. How do you think that helped the conversation? ____

____

Now choose one of the listening skills you would like to develop. Find a time to try it, and make sure to pay attention to how things go. Then write about your experience here: ____

____

____

... and more to do

Use your mindfulness skills the next time you have a conversation with someone. Really notice, without judgment, how that person reacts and responds to you during the conversation. Notice the words and tone of voice she or he uses. Notice hand gestures and where the person looks. Just observe the interaction and write about your experience:

____

____

____

How might this conversation have been different if you weren't fully paying attention?

____

____

____

____

reflecting on your experiences 35

for you to know

Reflection involves looking back on an experience and examining what it meant for you, both inside and outside. It might include noticing changes in the way you think or feel about something as a result of the experience. It can also result in increased awareness of things that are important to you, getting to know your strengths and challenges, or behaving differently. No matter what it brings up for you, reflection can help you identify important aspects of any experience and help you keep hold of them more fully.

Brittany got this workbook after she was diagnosed with bipolar disorder. It took her a while, but she did almost every activity in the book. She was determined to have the life she wanted; she had plans to go to college and get a job, and nothing was going to stop her! When she looked back on the experience of using the workbook, she noticed that she remembered some activities better than others and that some of the information had really stayed with her while other parts did not.

As she continued to reflect on this experience, she realized that some of the parts that stayed with her were the ones she had struggled with and wanted to improve. Other parts stuck with her because she found them interesting and they fit with how she liked to think about things. As she reflected on other changes, she noticed that she was taking her medication more regularly and that she was saying what was on her mind more. She decided that these changes were positive and that she was beginning to live according to her goals and values.

for you to do

Reflect on the experience of using this workbook. What parts come to mind?

____

____

What does remembering these parts of the book mean to you? Think about Brittany's experience if you feel stuck.

____

____

Hopefully you've already made some changes as a result of using this workbook. Some of these may be changes in how you think, feel, or act. Reflect on each of these separately and list the changes you've made. If you are having difficulty, ask someone you trust to reflect on the changes he or she has noticed. We've included some examples to help you.

Ways I am *thinking* differently:

- Drugs can be harmful, especially with my diagnosis.
- I can make changes in how I act in relationships.
- There are people who can help me if I'm in crisis.
- There are things I can do to manage my bipolar disorder.
- ____
- ____
- ____
- ____

Ways I am *feeling* differently:

- I feel less scared.
- I feel more hopeful.
- I still feel angry about all of this, but not as much.
- I feel calmer when I use mindfulness.
- ______________________________
- ______________________________
- ______________________________
- ______________________________

Ways I am *acting* differently:

- I am taking my medication more regularly.
- I am tuning into my breath more often.
- I am drinking a lot less alcohol.
- I am acting calmer even when I am having intense feelings.
- ______________________________
- ______________________________
- ______________________________
- ______________________________

... and more to do

Think about the changes you've listed above. What do these changes say to you about yourself?

___

___

___

More specifically, what skills, abilities, and qualities did you draw upon to do this?

- ☐ focus
- ☐ optimism
- ☐ ambition
- ☐ determination
- ☐ ___
- ☐ ___
- ☐ ___
- ☐ ___

continuing to move forward 36

for you to know

Moving forward means staying or getting on a path that fits your values and preferences for yourself. Moving forward means thinking, feeling, and behaving in ways that meet your needs and wants now and in the future. Change is often a part of this complex process. Sometimes change seems to happen on its own, and other times it seems to take tons of work and lots of time. If you plan for the changes you want to make, you are more likely to succeed in making them.

Brittany never really had to think about change until she was diagnosed with bipolar disorder. Up until a few months before, things had gone pretty smoothly for her. When she received the diagnosis, though, it seemed like everything was instantly different. She was told that she would have to make some significant changes in her life.

One thing Brittany wanted to work toward changing was her sleeping habits. She had always managed to function with only six hours of sleep. She liked to stay up chatting online with friends but had to be up early for school. She wanted to attend college and knew she had to do well in school. Getting more sleep was going to be an important part of staying well and succeeding in school, but she still wanted to be able to talk to her friends. To help her make the change, Brittany followed these steps:

Step 1: She listed the advantages and disadvantages of getting more sleep.

Advantages:

- I'll be able to manage my mood better.
- I'll be able to concentrate better at school.
- I'll get more done after school because I won't be as tired.

Disadvantages:

- I won't be able to talk to friends for as long.
- I might lose friends if I'm not talking to them as much.

Step 2: Since there were more advantages than disadvantages, she decided that the change was worthwhile. She prepared to make the change by writing down what she could do to get more sleep. If she had trouble coming up with ideas, she planned to do some research or ask for help.

- I have to decide what time I should go to bed. Ten p.m. is a good time because it would give me about nine hours of sleep.
- I'll ask Mom if we can have dinner earlier so I have more time afterward to get things done.
- I'll tell my friends that I won't be online as late and ask some of them to help me with this.
- I'll write down the reasons why I want to get to bed early on a piece of paper and put it where I can see it often.
- I'll set my alarm clock to remind me that it's time to start getting ready for bed.
- I'll be my own coach and have a good talk with myself if I start to lose my determination to make this change.
- I'll be gentle with myself if things don't go smoothly in the beginning.

Step 3: She kept on track by noticing how much better she felt with more sleep. She told herself:

- Even if I stay up late one night, it doesn't mean I've failed or can't make this change.
- I'll keep doing what works so that going to bed on time becomes part of my usual routine.

Step 4: If she stopped going to bed early, she got back on track (which is a typical and important part of change!).

- If for some reason I'm no longer going to bed early, even after I was able to do it for a while, I'll go back to an earlier step and repeat the process. I know I may feel disappointed or hopeless, but I will be kind to myself and remind myself this is a normal and important part of change.

Recognizing that change is a process of steps helped Brittany feel more confident, and her goal of getting more sleep seemed more manageable.

for you to do

Look back through this workbook. To continue to move forward in your life, what changes do you think you need to make but haven't started working on yet? For example, are you still not keeping track of your mood or working on your communication skills? There may be many, since you've just completed this workbook, so write down only the ones that really stand out to you.

______________________ ______________________

______________________ ______________________

______________________ ______________________

Think about how important these changes are to you. Rate each from 0 (not important at all) to 10 (very important). Write the number beside each item above.

Write down the change that you rated as the most important. If there is more than one, choose the one you want to start working on first.

____

____

____

Why do you think this change is so important? ______________________

____

____

____

Now, think about how confident you are that you'll be able to make this important change. On a scale of 0 (not at all confident) to 10 (very confident), how would you rate it? If you rated your confidence higher than 5, what helps you feel so confident about your ability to make this change? Hint: your skills, abilities, and resources may play a role.

____

____

If you rated your confidence 5 or less, what would help you to feel more confident? We've listed some ideas for you to consider:

- Ask for help.
- Give yourself permission to not have to do it perfectly or right away.
- Use this workbook to refresh your memory about the information or steps you can take.
- Tell yourself even small changes are helpful.
- ____
- ____
- ____

Choose one of these, try it, and notice what happens to your confidence. How would you rate it now? _______________

If you still don't feel more confident, try another one of the ideas listed above and keep at it!

... and more to do

Review these steps that Brittany followed in changing her sleep habits:

1. List the advantages and disadvantages of the change.
2. Use your list to decide whether you are going to make the change. If you are, write down your ideas for how to do it. If you have trouble coming up with ideas, do some research or ask someone you trust for ideas.
3. Keep on track by noticing how you feel as you go.
4. Remind yourself that change doesn't always go smoothly and, if necessary, go back to an earlier step.

On a separate piece of paper, write down your thoughts about what needs to happen at each step for you to make the change you want to make.

afterword

This book was written to help you develop your awareness of the influence bipolar disorder or mood swings can have over you and, more importantly, the influence you have over them. We've shared ideas and information with the aim of helping you to identify your skills and abilities and what you'd like to change, and then to actually make changes. However, we also know that *you* have knowledge and expertise. It will be important for you to draw upon your own knowledge and expertise in your efforts to limit the effects of your condition and live your preferred life. We hope this workbook has contributed to this process.

Sheri Van Dijk, MSW, is a mental health therapist in private practice at Southlake Regional Health Centre in Newmarket, ON, Canada. She specializes in the treatment of bipolar disorder and other psychiatric disorders using dialectical behavior therapy (DBT) and mindfulness practice. She is author of *The Dialectical Behavior Therapy Skills Workbook for Bipolar Disorder*. Visit her online at www.sherivandijk.com.

Photograph by K. Guindon

Karma Guindon, MSW, RSW, RMFT, is a clinical social worker and registered marriage and family therapist in private practice and at a child and family mental health program at Southlake Regional Health Centre in Newmarket, ON, Canada. She uses an integrative and collaborative therapeutic approach with the children, adolescents, adults, families, and couples who meet with her for psychotherapy. She is also in doctoral studies in social work at Wilfrid Laurier University in Kitchener, ON.